# SPEAKER

## LEADER

# CHAMPION

# SPEAKER
# LEADER
# CHAMPION

## SUCCEED AT WORK THROUGH THE
## POWER OF PUBLIC SPEAKING

JEREMEY DONOVAN
RYAN AVERY

New York  Chicago  San Francisco  Athens  London  Madrid
Mexico City  Milan  New Delhi  Singapore  Sydney  Toronto

1 2 3 4 5 6 7 8 9 0   DOC/DOC   1 2 0 9 8 7 6 5 4

ISBN      978-0-07-183104-8
MHID       0-07-183104-5

e-ISBN  978-0-07-183115-4
e-MHID       0-07-183115-0


Library of Congress Cataloging-in-Publication Data

Donovan, Jeremey.
    Speaker, leader, champion : succeed at work through the power of public speaking / by Jeremey Donovan and Ryan Avery.
        pages cm
    ISBN-13: 978-0-07-183104-8 (pbk.)
    ISBN-10: 0-07-183104-5 (pbk.)
    1. Public speaking. 2. Business presentations. 3. Business communication. I. Avery, Ryan. II. Title.
PN4193.B8D66 2014
808.5'1—dc23

                                                                          2013050217

McGraw-Hill Education books are available at special quantity discounts to use as premiums and sales promotions or for use in corporate training programs. To contact a representative, please visit the Contact Us pages at www.mhprofessional.com.

Toastmasters International, the Toastmasters International logo, and all other Toastmasters International trademarks and copyrights are the sole property of Toastmasters International. Used with permission.

# CONTENTS

# ACKNOWLEDGMENTS

It takes a community of leaders to write a book. We are indebted to our agent, Jackie Meyer, to our "secret" line editor, PJ Dempsey, and to the following individuals on the McGraw-Hill team for the magic they create behind the scenes: Chelsea Van der Gaag, Ann Pryor, Mary Glenn, Ron Martirano, and Janice Race.

A special thank-you to our editor extraordinaire, Casey Ebro. We almost *wanted* to keep revising this book because the guidance you gave us made the book 10 times better after every draft. You should be writing books about public speaking yourself; yet you humbly give your ideas freely so others look good, with no expectation of attribution.

This book would not have been possible without the guidance of the past Toastmasters World Champions of Public Speaking. We would like to especially acknowledge the individuals who guided us and generously shared permission to reprint their speeches: David Brooks, Mark Brown, Craig Valentine, Ed Tate, Darren LaCroix, Lance Miller, Randy Harvey, David Henderson, the estate of LaShunda Rundles, and Jock Elliott.

· · · · ·

I am grateful to the worldwide community of Toastmasters members and officers for believing in me, investing in me, and helping make one of my dreams come true. I owe a deep thank-you to District 7 Toastmasters. In addition, I have enjoyed visiting countless clubs and districts around the world that invited me to share my knowledge of how to improve communication skills. I look forward to visiting many more. Together, we are reminding people that their voice matters.

Randy Harvey, there are no words to express how much your mentorship means to me and to convey my appreciation for how you took me under your wing and then pushed me to fly on my own. Where would I be as a speaker without you?

Thank you to my mom, dad, sister, extended family, friends, and the team at Special Olympics Oregon. You have done more for me than you will ever know!

Chelsea, you are my dream. You amplify my life. Thank you for giving me inspiration when I need it most.

**—RA**

. . . . .

Over the years, I have had the honor of watching many great speakers in Toastmasters clubs around the world. I also delivered a few speeches of my own. Thank you to my fellow Toastmasters, past and present, who taught me by example and through constructive feedback. Joshua Reynolds and Grant Dubois dragged me kicking and screaming to the front of the room to deliver my first table topic. Josh and Grant, though our lives have taken us down different paths, thank you for starting my journey as a speaker. I am especially grateful to the members of my two home clubs, Greater Stamford Toastmasters and Gartner Toastmasters.

Last and most important, thank you to my loving and patient family.

**—JD**

# SPEAKER

# LEADER

# CHAMPION

# Gaining the Speaking Edge

Any one of a number of surveys conclusively finds that public speaking is intrinsically linked to business success. Among the most prominent is the one conducted annually by the National Association of Colleges and Employers. In its *Job Outlook 2013* survey of 244 employers, the "ability to verbally communicate with persons inside and outside the organization" was the number one skill (rated 4.63 on a 5-point scale) desired by employers in evaluating job candidates. The report states, "The ideal candidate is a good communicator who can make decisions and solve problems while working effectively in a team."

If you are still not convinced, consider the impact that public speaking ability has had on the authors of this book. Neither Jeremey, from generation X, nor Ryan, a millennial, was a born speaker. Nobody is. Yet both of us have parlayed countless hours of practice in a specific feedback-rich environment, Toastmasters. Jeremey leverages his public speaking skills to gain an edge in a traditional corporate environment, while Ryan uses his to excel as a professional speaker and entrepreneur.

In 1998, Jeremey transitioned from semiconductor engineering to semiconductor industry analysis. With that move, Jeremey needed to overcome his social anxiety and learn to speak in public to build his career. What probably sounds like a small change to you was a gargantuan leap for him: he could no longer hide in his cubicle, because his job required him to speak to senior executives and to present to large audiences.

Jeremey walked into his first Toastmasters meeting during lunch one day in Gartner Inc.'s office in San Jose, California. He took great care to sit in the back of the room. This went on for many meetings until two colleagues, Joshua Reynolds and Grant Dubois, dragged him kicking and screaming to the front of the room to deliver his first table topic, a one- to two-minute impromptu speech. It was a horrifying experience for Jeremey—and for his audience.

Over the course of 15 years in Toastmasters, Jeremey's growth as a speaker fueled his growth as a business leader. Today, Jeremey is group vice president of marketing for a $1.6 billion company, where he leads a 50-person global team.

While Jeremey joined Toastmasters to save his job, Ryan was drawn to the organization in late 2010 to hone his interviewing skills. Jobless and broke, Ryan needed his father to pay his membership dues of less than $100 for the first year. In his first Toastmasters meeting, Ryan was stunned by the extent to which strangers offered to help with communication and leadership advice. Ryan's efforts bore fruit a few months later when he accepted a position as a marketing manager at Special Olympics Oregon.

Ryan still had a lot of work to do to improve his verbal communication skills. Within weeks of beginning the job, he gave his first television interview to promote an upcoming event. Later that night, Ryan watched in embarrassment, counting the number of times he said "like" during two minutes on camera. Determined not to repeat the mistake, Ryan practiced his professional presentations in his Toastmasters club before high-stakes speaking engagements.

At the end of a two-hour YouTube-watching marathon one lazy Saturday morning in late 2011, Ryan saw a video of a competitor in the Toastmasters World Championship of Public Speaking and decided to compete. While Toastmasters officially has two tracks, one for speaking and one for leadership, Ryan found that the pressure and repetitive refinement offered by the unofficial "competition track" advanced his speaking ability at an exponential rate. At each level of the 2012 contest, he worked harder by practicing and integrating expert feedback. His training paid off at work, too, with a promotion to director in June 2012. Two months later, at age 25, Ryan became the youngest-ever Toastmasters World Champion of Public Speaking. Not bad for someone born into the "um, like, you know" generation.

The next morning, Ryan woke up to 269 e-mails with offers to speak all around the world. While his employer provided support and flexibility, Ryan recognized that trying to do two things well was not going to allow him to become great at either. In early 2013, he became a full-time professional speaker and trainer to help others of his generation improve their communication skills.

We can confidently say that our ever-developing public speaking ability is the single biggest factor in whatever success we have had. But we are just two examples and by no means the pinnacle of business success. One need not look far to find better examples of famous Toastmasters, including Chris Matthews, host of *Hardball with Chris Matthews*, Nancy Brinker, founder of the Susan G. Komen Breast Cancer Foundation, and Paul Oreffice, former president and CEO of Dow Chemical.

For the benefit of the uninitiated and in the organization's own words, "Toastmasters International is a non-profit educational organization that teaches public speaking and leadership skills through a worldwide network of meeting locations." As of July 1, 2013, this network includes more than 292,000 individuals who gather as often as every week at one of 14,350 clubs across 122 countries.

Toastmasters was founded by Ralph C. Smedley at the turn of the twentieth century. After Mr. Smedley graduated from Illinois Wesleyan University in 1903, he took a job as director of education for the Young Men's Christian Association (YMCA) chapter in Bloomington, Illinois. Noticing that the patrons lacked polish in various speaking endeavors, including giving toasts at banquets, he formed a club where young men could take turns giving short speeches that were immediately evaluated by peers. As Mr. Smedley moved westward across the United States from YMCA to YMCA, he formed new Toastmasters clubs, attracting YMCA patrons and local business professionals seeking to improve their interpersonal and business communication skills. Unfortunately, each club disbanded after his departure.

When Mr. Smedley arrived in 1924 as general secretary of the YMCA in Santa Ana, California, he again started a Toastmasters club, but this time, the club and the concepts endured. Within two years, a second club was formed in nearby Anaheim. By 1938, 100 clubs had been chartered in the United States and abroad. Individual memberships vaulted past 100,000 in October 1982 and have continued to grow at a healthy clip through the decades.

Though Toastmasters did not open membership to women until 1973, it is now one of the most diverse public service organizations in existence. It is gender blind (52 percent of members are female, and 48 percent are male), age blind (the average member age is 45.8 years, but 25 percent of members are ages 18–24), income blind, education blind, and disability blind. The same goes for race, religion, and sexual orientation. Every person with an interest in improving public speaking or leadership skills is welcome.

Today, Toastmasters has little or nothing to do with actually giving toasts. It is not an instructor-led course and has no set enrollment dates. Instead, the program is almost entirely self-directed and consists of three components: a communications track, a leadership track, and a competition track. While most members pursue only the communications track, others participate in all three concurrently. For less than $100 per year, the return on investment is nearly infinite for those who are committed to self-improvement. The regular practice that Toastmasters affords helps you continually hone your speaking skills, especially the ability to cope with fear.

Toastmasters teaches individuals *both* how to deliver informational personal speeches and how to deliver persuasive presentations in a business environment. The initial requirement of the Toastmasters speaking track is completing 10 speeches in the *Competent Communication* manual. The manual begins with speeches geared toward giving novice, often terrified, speakers the confidence needed to speak in front of a room full of strangers. To make that achievement possible, speakers are encouraged to share informational stories about their personal or professional lives. After facing their fear, speakers move on to getting comfortable with specific aspects of their verbal and nonverbal delivery. For the first eight speeches, content is indeed subordinate to delivery. However, the emphasis shifts in the final two speeches, which call for delivering persuasive and then inspirational content. As speakers move on to the advanced communication requirements, they learn to conquer technical presentations, facilitating discussion, and a set of common speeches by management.

Going to a Toastmasters meeting is a bit like going to the gym or to a yoga class. Very well intentioned people suggest that you repetitively lift extreme weights and assume ridiculous poses that would look artificial in other environments. The point is to build strength, flexibility, and muscle memory so that you can go about your daily life with more grace and power. Once you learn to push the limits of theatricality and to mostly eliminate filler words, both verbal and nonverbal delivery become second nature, allowing you to easily go into a business presentation fully focused on content.

Toastmasters evaluations challenge speakers to grow. Distinguished Toastmaster David Hobson summarized the feedback ethos of the organization:

> *Criticism is easy; we hear it all the time in every walk of life. However, criticism is the language of cowards. Criticism is negative. Even a critique (a term used by non-Toastmasters), being a critical analysis, almost sounds like a put-down. Evaluation on the other hand considers the value, the good aspects, and adds value with helpful suggestions for improvement.*[1]

Criticism is a very important part of the Toastmasters speaking and leadership journey, but it is delivered in the form of a balanced, constructive, and supportive speech evaluation. An ineffective criticism would curtly inform the speaker: "Your eye contact was poor." In contrast, an effective evaluation provides the constructive feedback necessary for growth as a speaker. The Toastmasters way is to say: "I noticed that you were scanning the audience as you spoke. Next time, consider holding eye contact for three seconds with individuals in a random pattern across the room."

Our intent is to fill the gap between the lessons of the Toastmasters experience and those of a professional speaking coach. To accomplish that, we have deconstructed and codified the content and delivery practices of 11 winners of the Toastmasters World Championship of Public Speaking. While these experts are masters of inspirational storytelling, their techniques apply to all types of public speaking situations.

To gain an edge at work by applying the lessons you learn in this book, you do not need to be a Toastmaster, but we do encourage you to join the organization in order to practice in its safe, feedback-rich, low-cost environment. For those of you who join Toastmasters and decide to compete in the World Championship of Public Speaking, we provide a specialized set of bonus tips at the end of the book.

While many how-to books include end-of-chapter exercises, our tips are intended to double as exercises. As you read a tip that resonates with your development as a speaker, practice it until you achieve a reasonable degree of mastery and move on to the next one. We have also combined all our tips into a quick reference guide at the back of the book.

Let's get started, so that you become our next example of a person whose career accelerated to warp speed through the power of public speaking.

## CHAPTER 1

# Selecting a Topic

### TIP 1: Speak to serve.

Second only to managing fear, selecting a compelling topic is your biggest challenge. Even world champion Lance Miller (2005)* was not immune: "When I was trying to find messages to use as speech topics, I was so frustrated because nothing really bad had ever happened to me. I came from a good family; I had a good education; I had good jobs. Where is the inspiration in that?" Lance's question reveals that purpose selection precedes topic selection.

There are striking parallels between finding your professional purpose and finding the purpose of a speech. Nearly every book or article ever written about finding your purpose offers identical yet profound advice—to discover your true calling, pick a vocation that lies at the intersection of three considerations: what is valued by others, what you are great at, and what you would be willing to do even if money were no object. The stakes are higher in speech topic selection because getting your professional purpose wrong just wastes your time, but getting your speech purpose wrong wastes

---

* Throughout the book, the date in parentheses indicates the year the speaker won the Toastmasters World Championship of Public Speaking.

everyone's time. For that reason, the starting point for selecting the purpose of a speech is *what is valued by others.*

The value of a speech to others lies in the impact it has on each listener's knowledge, actions, and feelings. Toastmasters calls this the *general purpose* of a speech, prescribing that every speech must accomplish one of the following purposes: to inform, to persuade, to entertain, or to inspire. Though most speeches blend multiple elements, every good speech is defined by a dominant general purpose.

Speaking to inform is the easiest, though least engaging, form of public speaking in both personal and professional environments. Many typical work presentations, including budget reviews and project status updates, fall into the informational category.

Speaking to inspire is valuable in personal settings and business settings. Classic workplace examples are a CEO outlining her vision for the coming year at an all-company meeting and a sales leader announcing a new quarterly bonus plan. However, speaking to inspire is even more important for associates who lack positional authority. To enlist immediate colleagues and cross-functional peers, you must sell your ideas and inspire people to believe that supporting you is good for them and for the company.

Speaking to entertain is mostly confined to personal settings and casual work conversation. However, one example in a formal work environment is delivering an after-dinner address at a holiday party. For the most part, entertaining speeches are not intended to have a lasting impact on an audience; such speeches are designed solely for pure enjoyment.

Speaking to persuade is the most valuable general purpose. A persuasive speech convinces someone to change a belief, commit time and money to your idea, or compel action. Perhaps you are a retail manager seeking to persuade employees to greet customers in a particular way that is proved to increase sales. Or you are a graphic designer trying to convince your client to engage you for his next project. Either way, you begin with an informational component that provides background, move into a problem-solving element that reviews potential solutions, and end with the persuasive punch that proves your recommendation is valuable.

What is the purpose of your speech?

## TIP 2: Choose a single core message that serves your audience's needs and interests.

Finalists in the World Championship of Public Speaking know that their audiences, including the judges, expect to be inspired even though the contest rules do not mandate purpose. After competing and losing for 13 years, Lance Miller made a breakthrough when he stopped thinking about himself and started thinking about his audience. "I asked myself, 'What have I learned? What has made a difference in my life that I would want to share with the audience?' It struck me that if we just validated each other, by looking for what is right rather than for what is wrong, then the world would be a much better place."

Toastmasters recommends that all speeches not only have a dominant *general* purpose but also have a single *special purpose*. Rather than special purpose, we prefer the term *core message* or *central idea* because each term better reflects the goal that speakers be clear about *what* they want the audience to know, feel, or do. Novice speakers tend to cram in too many core messages. As illustrated in his speech, Lance stayed laser focused on his single audience-centric idea of validating others.

*Each of the championship speeches featured in this book is accompanied by a table that includes four vital statistics. As you read each speech, see how the central message serves as the spine to which every word relates. Notice the breadth and depth of storytelling that the speakers are able to convey in the brief duration and measured words-per-minute pace. Finally, seek out the frequent and delightful humor that appears in support of the message, regardless of how serious the subject matter is.*

# The Ultimate Question (2005)

| | |
|---|---|
| **Central message(s)** | Love |
| **Duration** | 7.30 minutes |
| **Words per minute** | 131 |
| **Laughs per minute** | 2.19 |

### (INTRODUCTION)

The ultimate question, that question that has plagued man since the dawn of time, and that question that each and every one of us must ask at some point in our life, do you validate?

### (PART 1)

Mr. Chairman, fellow Toastmasters and friends, I was 26 years old. I was living in a small town in Indiana. I had a job I didn't like. I hadn't had a date in three years, and I had a couple of room-mates named Mom and Dad.

I felt like my life was going nowhere so I took control. I left my home and my family, and I headed to Los Angeles to start over. Six months later, I had a job I didn't like. I was dating a girl who was trying to make me better by pointing out all of my faults. And I had a couple of roommates that made "Dumb and Dumber" look like Einstein and Oppenheimer.

I had changed everything in my life, but nothing had changed. I still felt like I was going nowhere.

### (PART 2)

And then, one day after a business meeting, all I wanted to do was get my parking validated. And I walked over to the receptionist and said, "Excuse me, do you validate?"

She looked up and said, "Well, yes I do. You have a lovely smile."

Showing her the ticket, I said, "No, I was just in a meeting with your boss; do you validate?"

And she said, "Well, let me compliment you on what a fine choice of business associates you have."

Catching on I said, "You have such a keen sense of humor, I'm going to go tell your boss how lucky he is to have you out here."

And she goes, "Give me that ticket." She took her little machine, and she went *cha-ching*, and as she handed it back, she looked at me and she said, "There's something special about you."

I took the ticket and headed for the elevator, but I stopped and I turned around and just said, "Thank you."

I don't know how long it had been since I'd felt validated. Her words stayed with me all the way home. And as I was looking at my life, I started to wonder how long it had been since I'd validated somebody else. I wanted to do that. I wanted to make people feel good, but I felt that I needed to be important. I needed to be successful, so that when I said something to somebody, it meant something to them, but that receptionist had just made my day. Heck, she made my month. With one little *cha-ching*, she stamped my ticket, and I thought I can do that.

## (PART 3)

So, I went home to see Dumb and Dumber. These guys were constantly bringing people back to the apartment. It was driving me nuts, but I went in and I said, "You make friends faster than anybody I have ever seen, and that is a gift." To see their faces, I swear they got smarter right before my eyes. *Cha-ching.*

I went to see my girlfriend, and I thanked her for caring enough about me that she wanted to see me be as good as I could be. You know what? She got nicer. *Cha-ching.*

I went to work, and I thanked my boss for hiring me. He'd done me a favor, and I started to enjoy my work a lot more. *Cha-ching*.

I used to think I had to be important before I could validate other people. I used to look at people as obstacles to my success, but what I discovered was I became important when I validated other people. I became important to that person and that person. People were the pathway to my success. I started trying to find something I could stamp on everybody I met. That little piece of goodness, that little piece of rightness. Just a little *cha-ching*.

### (CONCLUSION)

I started to feel like a superhero. Underneath this mild-mannered exterior was a blue and red spandex suit with a giant V on the chest. Yes, I was The Validator.

When things would get tense, they'd tighten up, I'd come in, and *cha-ching, cha-ching, cha-ching*! I had plenty of ink. I'd hear people say, "Who was that man?"

"I don't know, but I heard this *cha-ching* and suddenly I feel so much better now."

And then I figured it out. Do you know what's wrong with the world? Do you know what's wrong with me? Do you know what's wrong with you? Who cares!

The question is, What is right with the world? What is right with me? What is right with you? The common denominator of all humanity is the fact that we are human. We are, by nature, imperfect. It takes no special talent to find an imperfection in another person.

But every person goes through life wanting to be right, wanting to be valuable. Find that. Bring it out in them.

I started to discover in my life that I got what I validated. I found out that I brought out the goodness, the value in others by validating that.

> We have a lot of problems in this world, but I've learned that there is not a problem that exists between a parent and a child, between a husband and a wife, between a worker and his employer, or between races, cultures, or nations that does not stem directly from an inability or an unwillingness to validate the rightness, the value, and the goodness in another.
>
> This is the ultimate question. Do you validate, but this is not what's important. What's important is can you *cha-* [Audience: *ching*]? Can you *cha-* [Audience: *ching*]? Can you *cha-* [Audience: *ching*]? You've been a great audience.

## TIP 3:  Choose a single, inspirational core theme rooted in an eternal truth.

Beyond having to meet timing and originality requirements, Toastmasters world championship contestants are free to do and say pretty much anything. That said, of the 100 possible points that can be awarded, 30 points are associated with topic selection, with the first 15 points devoted to "Effectiveness: Achievement of Purpose, Interest, Reception" and the remaining 15 to "Speech Value: Ideas, Logic, Original Thought." Interestingly, the "Purpose" part of the "Achievement of Purpose" is not defined in any official rule book.

Most winning speeches are inspirational at their core, though they have a strong dose of motivation as well as inspiration. In a nutshell, that means the International Speech Contest calls for a seven-minute secular sermon centered on reminding the audience about an eternal truth or virtue. One often hears of the seven heavenly virtues, but there are scores of virtues that are relevant to our daily lives. The chart that follows provides a partial list of virtues that make great fodder for inspirational speeches of all kinds.

## Eternal Virtues for Inspirational Speech Topic Selection

Action (incl. drive, ambition, risk taking)

Authenticity (incl. individuality, self-expression)

Balance

Calm (incl. tranquillity)

Charity (incl. generosity, sharing, benevolence)

Companionship (incl. friendship)

Compassion (incl. understanding, acceptance, tolerance, empathy, warmth, caring)

Connectedness (incl. cooperation, community)

Contentment

Confidence (incl. assertiveness)

Courage (incl. valor, bravery)

Creativity (incl. ingenuity, originality)

Curiosity (incl. learning)

Forgiveness (incl. mercy)

Gratitude (incl. politeness, courtesy)

Honesty (incl. integrity, sincerity)

Humility (incl. modesty, discretion)

Humor (incl. joyfulness)

Justice (incl. fairness, impartiality)

Knowledge (incl. wisdom, perspective)

Leadership

Love (incl. kindness, appreciation, faithfulness, loyalty, devotion)

Mindfulness (incl. perspective, presence, silence)

Optimism (incl. hopefulness, enthusiasm, positivity)

Passion (incl. enthusiasm, vitality)

Perseverance (incl. resilience, persistence, industriousness, determination)

Responsibility (incl. citizenship, trust, integrity)

Self-control (incl. temperance, patience)

Spirituality (incl. faith, belief)

Vulnerability

In the 17-year period from 1995 to 2011, variations on the theme of *love* were the most popular, appearing five times. *Perseverance* was the second most common, having been revisited three times. *Mindfulness* and *action* have each found their way to the stage twice. Rounding out the list with one appearance each were *compassion, creativity, self-expression, hope,* and *tolerance.*

## TIP 4: Design your speech to have an impact.

Knowing your purpose and your core message is necessary but not sufficient. In addition, speeches must also have a compelling reason to exist. The message must motivate the members of your audience by illuminating *why* they should think, feel, or act differently. A winning speech can be summarized in a succinct, confident assertion that reads, "I will (*purpose*) my audience to (*core message*) so that (*impact*)." The digested version of Lance Miller's speech is, "I will inspire my fellow Toastmasters to validate the goodness in others so that the world becomes a safer and more loving place." As you can see, the impact is an audience-centric benefit.

This principle applies as strongly in business as it does to Toastmasters. Let's illustrate this with four examples—some as lofty as Lance's, others more mundane—one for each of the four purposes:

- I will inform my boss about the status of my project so that she feels comfortable with the progress we are making.

- I will persuade our sales force to use the new customer relationship management system so that they win more business.

- I will inspire my front-line service team to delight our customers so that they can build trust-based, value-added relationships.

- I will entertain my fellow employees and their guests so they can relax and enjoy themselves.

## TIP 5: Talk about subjects you know.

Thus far, we have addressed only the first of the three intersecting considerations, what is valued by others. Now we turn to the second consideration, *what you are great at*. The speaking parallel of doing what you are great at is speaking about topics you are deeply knowledgeable about.

Nelson Mandela is widely regarded as one of the most powerful and influential speakers of the twentieth century. His opening statement in his trial on April 20, 1964, on charges of sabotage established the stakes in the long struggle against apartheid. Addressing the judge, he concluded as follows:

> *During my lifetime I have dedicated myself to this struggle of the African people. I have fought against white domination, and I have fought against black domination. I have cherished the ideal of a democratic and free society in which all persons live together in harmony and with equal opportunities. It is an ideal which I hope to live for and to achieve. But if needs be, it is an ideal for which I am prepared to die.*[1]

This speech was powerful because of his particular circumstances and his depth of knowledge and experience. Though it is an extreme, if not ridiculous, example, imagine if Nelson Mandela had introduced a new consumer technology such as the iPhone. Conversely, imagine, just as absurdly, Steve Jobs speaking to end unjust racial segregation in South Africa, a cause for which he was not known to have passion. It is less important to be an expert speaker than it is to be an expert who speaks.

## TIP 6: Thoroughly research your topic.

Outside of the World Championship of Public Speaking, presenters rarely have the luxury of telling a personal story. More often, speakers are called upon to present research findings and recommendations.

Set time in your calendar for research. What gets calendared gets done. Juggling family, work, and Toastmasters is no small task. Strive to conduct as much research as you can to achieve your goal given the amount of time and resources that you have available.

Explore a range of sources. Most presentations rely solely on secondary research that involves gathering and synthesizing existing information rather than collecting original data. In the past, this meant a trip to the library to comb through books, encyclopedias, newspapers, magazines, and journals. Today, a far vaster cache of sources is easily accessible on the Internet. Of course, even the Internet is just one among many repositories of information. For higher-stakes presentations, primary research is best. Primary research is the direct collection of information from experiments, surveys, or business transaction data. In the hard sciences, such experiments often take place in the laboratory. In business, primary research more often borrows social sciences techniques, including one-on-one interviews, surveys, focus groups, and small field tests often referred to as "pilots."

Be an unbiased anthropologist. There is a dizzying array of biases that cause people to make errors in decision making. Among them, confirmation bias is perhaps the most dangerous. Confirmation bias refers to the tendency to search for information that confirms our beliefs and to ignore information that challenges our beliefs. The best way to combat this decision-making error is to observe the world with an anthropologist's eye and actively try to prove your beliefs wrong during the research process.

Always document your work and cite your sources, whether you are conducting primary or secondary research. Legally and ethically, it is the right thing to do. But there are more direct personal benefits. When you cite sources, you boost your credibility. You need not go through excruciatingly detailed biographies of your sources; provide just enough to orient your listener. For instance, you might cite a secondary source as, "In a 2013 study conducted by Dr. Who at Johns Hopkins University, . . ." Or if you are setting up your findings from primary research, you might say, "My recommendations today are based on interviews with 100 customers in New York City."

Where possible, the proper way to conduct secondary research is to read the original primary research on a topic. Be careful about referencing a secondary source without fact checking. This is how urban legends are born. Consider the following cautionary tale:

Many public speaking experts and coaches cite the statistic that communication is 7 percent content, 38 percent vocal tone, and 55 percent body language. Precious few cite or even know where this came from. Fewer still bother to read the actual pair of 1967 studies conducted by Mehrabian, Ferris, and Wiener. Had people referred to the primary research, they would have found that the studies involved the reactions of test subjects to single spoken words. The studies were designed to estimate the impact of content, vocal tone, and body language on how listeners assessed a speaker's feelings of liking, neutrality, and disliking. Hence, applying this research to a normal conversation, let alone a full presentation, is a flawed misinterpretation. Dr. Mehrabian himself later wrote, "Unless a communicator is talking about their feelings or attitudes, these equations are not applicable."

## TIP 7:  Respect your audience's knowledge and intellect.

When delivering either a Toastmasters speech or a business speech, tune the complexity of the topic, language, and supporting detail to the knowledge level of the audience. Always speak directly to the people in your audience and never down or over their heads.

Lance Miller has the following advice for speakers who put themselves on a pedestal: "Humility and sincerity are what make great speakers and great speeches. Humility means you are talking eye to eye with your audience. I see people go into this authoritative posture, talking down to their audience. Their style becomes: 'I command you to think this way!' It is better to appreciate that your audience is made up of brilliant people—probably smarter than you are."

While Lance is right to view the members of the audience as equals, take care not to assume that they always share your depth of knowledge. For the most part, Lance's diverse audience could understand all his references with one possible exception. Consider his line "And I had a couple of roommates that made *Dumb and Dumber* look like Einstein and Oppenheimer." The popular movie

*Dumb and Dumber* was well embedded in the social consciousness, as it had been released only a few months before. Similarly, everyone could reasonably be expected to know who Albert Einstein was. However, it is likely that only the older people in the audience would know J. Robert Oppenheimer, the leader of the Manhattan Project and often called the father of the atomic bomb.

The importance of speaking at your audience's knowledge level is even greater for speakers in business settings. You will deliver most of your presentations to more senior people. Consequently, your natural inclination may be to show off your knowledge. However, most executives (who are generally *less* knowledgeable than you are about your subject) prefer that you speak to them as peers in simple, clear language.

## TIP 8:  Speak with authenticity.

Our exploration of the parallels between professional purpose and speech purpose ends with the third consideration, *what you would be willing to do even if money were no object.* The public speaking analogy is sharing with others the ideas that inspire you. When you are moved, you move your audience. Passion for your content is the heart and soul of authenticity. Audiences can detect conviction just by watching and listening to a speaker.

Inevitably, you will be called upon to deliver a presentation, especially at work, that does not stir your soul. Don't force it by pretending to be passionate, since false conviction is just as toxic as anemic conviction. Just speak the way you feel. If, in the extreme, you are asked to speak on a topic that you do *not* believe in, see if you can pass the opportunity to somebody who does.

When you speak about subjects you are deeply passionate about to individuals you care about, the speaking part comes easy. This is equally as true in business settings as it is in social settings. You can see this philosophy at work in how Lance Miller drafted his speech: "For me, the contest was a journey of self-discovery and self-worth.

You need to look at your life and define who you are. We go through life and get defined by our family and friends. We end up trying to be who they want us to be instead of who we want to be. When you can figure out who you are, then you have something of value to give the world through your words."

Lance Miller wore genuine interest—for his message and for his audience—on his sleeve. You feel it when he says, "I don't know how long it had been since I'd felt validated. Her words stayed with me all the way home. And as I was looking at my life, I started to wonder how long it had been since I'd validated somebody else. I wanted to do that."

People who acquire public speaking techniques often follow one of two paths. Some adopt a stiff, conservative persona devoid of emotion with a style that is almost too polished. Others artificially amp themselves up to unbridled, evangelical passion. Both types are guilty of forgetting to be the same person onstage as offstage. Lance showed true charisma by expressing genuine passion. He spoke to the people in his audience as equals traveling the same road.

Lance also made himself vulnerable to his audience by sharing his mistakes, challenges, and failures: "I had changed everything in my life, but nothing had changed. I still felt like I was going nowhere." His story was about an important epiphany in his journey through life, a life with past success and failure as well as opportunities and challenges ahead.

· · · · ·

Any speech you deliver should be on a sufficiently narrow topic at the intersection of what is valuable to your audience, what you are deeply knowledgeable about, and what you believe in passionately.

The next chapter explores how to structure a topic elegantly to deliver a winning speech at Toastmasters, at work, or in a personal setting.

## CHAPTER 2

# Organizing a Speech

**TIP 9:** Use an organizing framework to make it easy for an audience to grasp the message.

The *Competent Communication* manual, the starting point in the Toastmasters communications track, provides a fairly comprehensive set of frameworks for structuring speeches, including topical, spatial, causal, comparative, problem-solution, and chronological. Each framework is best suited for one or more of the four general purposes of informing, persuading, entertaining, and inspiring. The most important consideration is choosing a framework that makes it easy for your audience to grasp your core message.

**TIP 10:** Use the topical framework for informative speeches.

Topical speeches follow the classic introduction-body-conclusion structure where the points that constitute the body are classified using the same plural noun. For example, in a topical speech entitled "3 Daily Habits Guaranteed to Shed Pounds," the plural noun is *habits*. While topical, or informative, speeches are the mainstay of Toastmasters meetings, very few speeches with this framework have won the World Championship of Public Speaking. The bodies of most topical speeches consist of three main points, although there is no hard-and-fast rule.

Spatial speeches are a subtype of topical speeches in which the plural noun representing the main points in the body is *physical* locations. Speeches entitled "Our Three Most Profitable Stores" and "The Most Beautiful Vacation Spots in the World" are examples.

Causal speeches are another subtype of topical speeches in which the plural noun representing the main point is either *causes* or *effects*. Consider a speech titled "Reducing Shoplifting in Our Stores." The introduction frames the effect: losses from shoplifting have doubled from 2 to 4 percent of inventory in the past year. The body explores the causes: broken security cameras, high unemployment in the community, and fewer employees in stores. The conclusion recalls the effect and restates the causes. (If the conclusion included a recommendation to fix the issue, then the speech framework would be problem-solution rather than causal, a concept we will return to later.) If the introduction included the causes, the body would explore its effects: increased shoplifting, lower cash receipts due to employee theft from registers, and mayhem in the aisles.

### TIP 11:  Preview your core message, grab attention, and provide a road map in your introduction.

Jock Elliott's speech "Just So Lucky" (2011) is among the few topical speeches to have won the world championship, partly because the speech transcended description and inspired his audience. Let's deconstruct it to uncover best practices for developing an exceptional presentation. Most of his techniques apply equally well to each of the other speech frameworks. We begin by analyzing his introduction.

# Just So Lucky (2011)

| | |
|---|---|
| **Central message(s)** | Love |
| **Duration** | 6.78 minutes |
| **Words per minute** | 109 |
| **Laughs per minute** | 1.47 |

### (INTRODUCTION)

Mr. Contest Chairman, ladies and gentlemen, if I joined Twitter or Facebook, I could have hundreds of brand-new friends just like that. But how many of them would roll out of bed at three o'clock in the morning and come to my aid if I needed them? Probably not one.

So, who can I count on? John Lau says in his Facebook page that "Everyone has a best friend at each stage of their life. Only a lucky few have the same one." Well, I'm just so lucky because I have three best friends, and here they are: the friends of my blood, the friends of my times, and the friends of my heart.

In his brief introduction, Jock previewed his core message "the power of genuine friendship." Audiences have a right to know early in your speech what you are speaking about and why they should pay attention. The major choice you face lies in how directly you state your message and its benefits. If your message is noncontentious, state it as directly as possible. In contrast, if your audience is likely to reject your message, then you need to plant a tiny seed and then build your case. Jock's message of friendship is readily acceptable, so he took the direct approach. Jock had another reason to reveal his core message quickly: "As a listener, I am more than happy for a point to emerge a long way into the speech as long as it is going somewhere. However, the judges have to hang their judging criteria on a point. They need to see your message fairly early or at least have a useful departure point."

He ensured this message affected his audience on multiple levels when he shared with us, "For many years, I missed the point. I was probably too academic. I was passionate about what I was talking about, but I was obsessed with issues that did not have an emotional resonance. Ultimately, you have to touch your audience both intellectually and emotionally."

When delivering a presentation, you want to connect with every member of the audience. Jock grabbed his audience's attention with a provocative question: "But how many of them would roll out of bed at three o'clock in the morning and come to my aid if I needed them?"

In his introduction, Jock provided a road map to help his audience locate where he was in the progression of his speech. He said, "Well, I'm just so lucky because I have three best friends, and here they are: the friends of my blood, the friends of my times, and the friends of my heart." This sentence is a very literal application of a common public speaking mantra: "Tell them what you are going to tell them. Tell them. Tell them what you told them." We tend to prefer a more subtle variation on the first part of the mantra, "Tease them with what you are going to tell them." Had Jock followed this modification, he would have said, "Well, I'm just so lucky because I have three best friends," and refrained from stating the three types. Then he would have revealed each type as he moved through the body of his speech. This approach keeps the audience members in suspense while they simultaneously listen and await the satisfying unveiling of each type of friend.

### TIP 12: Open with a provocative question, a shocking statement, or a personal story.

Asking a provocative question, as Jock Elliott did in 2011, is one of the three highly effective openings we recommend. Jock was in good company with the champions from 2005, 2001, and 1992 who also opened with a provocative question. In fact, Lance Miller (2005) even titled his speech "The Ultimate Question." He connected getting a parking ticket validated with empowering others by expressing appreciation for their strengths rather than focusing on their weaknesses. He began:

> *The ultimate question, that question that has plagued man since the dawn of time, and that question that each and every one of us must ask at some point in our life, do you validate?*

Shocking statements most frequently rely on statistics, although they can also express strong opinions that challenge conventional wisdom. The important thing is that the statement must trigger a range of audience emotions. If you share a "what," then people will have a burning need to fill in the gaps on why, how, when, and where.

Since the shocking statement opener has not appeared in a winning Toastmasters speech, let's turn to the world of the TED conference. In his TED2010 talk, celebrity chef and child-nutrition advocate Jamie Oliver used exactly this recipe in his opening. Listen to how he started:

> *Sadly, in the next eighteen minutes when I do our chat, four Americans that are alive will be dead from the food that they eat. My name is Jamie Oliver. I am thirty-four years old. I am from Essex in England and for the last seven years I have worked fairly tirelessly to save lives in my own way. I am not a doctor; I'm a chef. I don't have expensive equipment, or medicine. I use information and education. I profoundly believe that the power of food has a primal place in our homes that binds us to the best bits of life.*

Chef Oliver captured his audience by sharing *what* is happening—people are dropping like flies from the food they eat in the same modern nation as his audience. No doubt most of the audience members were wondering if they would survive lunch! Such is the power of a shocking statistic that is deeply and personally relevant to the audience. People have four core needs: physical health and safety; love and belonging; desire and self-interest; and hope in a brighter future. Jamie went primal, life and death, and had his audience waiting with bated breath to find out why this is happening and to learn how to stay alive.

The personal story, the most common opening of public speaking world champions, builds an immediate emotional connection. In 26 years, 19 champions opened with a story: 14 with a personal story and the remaining 5 with stories about others. Vikas Jhingran (2007) allowed his audience to relive one of the defining moments of his life:

> *My hands were shaking. My throat was dry. In my hand was a letter that was going to change my life. Would it be for the better or worse? The answer was inside. I stared at the return address, MIT, Massachusetts Institute of Technology, the graduate school of my dreams. Would it begin with congratulations or "you've got to be kidding." The answer was inside.*

Of the five winners who opened with someone else's story, Mark Hunter (2009) conjured Don Quixote, the man of La Mancha, to personify what it means to idealistically champion the rights of others. Though he quickly shifted to personal storytelling, he integrated subtle chivalric references throughout the body of his speech, including references to a lance, armor, and horse. His approach of using repeated symbols, known in screenwriting theory as a thematic image system, added depth and sophistication.

Telling nonpersonal stories is a relic of bygone times and most likely would not win today. Arabella Bengson (1986) opened with *Pygmalion*. Harold Patterson (1987) opened with an exchange between the artists Henri Matisse and Pierre-Auguste Renoir. David Ross (1991) described a metaphysical train that transports people to success. Otis Williams Jr. (1993) referenced Thomas Edison. Only the earliest two, Ms. Bengson and Mr. Patterson, never transitioned into personal storytelling.

Though you see many speakers today open with quotes, it is no longer considered a sophisticated approach. People want to hear *your* words. It is, however, still acceptable to include quotes within the body of a speech. The last time a speech that opened with a quote won was in 1995, when Mark Brown used, "You never get a second chance to make a first impression." The only other instance was in 1990, when David Brooks quoted the title of Thomas Wolfe's novel *You Can't Go Home Again*.

### TIP 13: Use parallel transitional words and phrases to orient your audience.

Notice how Jock used transitional words as he transitioned into the body of his speech:

**(PART 1)**

First, over here, the friends of my blood. That is my family. My mom and dad, my brothers and sisters, my children. This is an old friendship forged from birth. A lifelong link between my past and my future. Of course, we have had our differences, just like every family. But I am just so lucky because we got over those. And anyway, if you cannot shout at your brother and sister, who can you shout at? And blood is thicker than water. And no one is thicker than my brother.

There are many transitional words and phrases, but ordinal numbers (*first, second, third,* etc.) are the most common. Jock launched into part 1 of the body of his speech with, "First, over here, the friends of my blood." In part 2, he began, "Now here, we have the friends of my times." And in part 3, he continued, "And finally here, we have the friends of my heart." Since we are nitpickers, we wish Jock had replaced "First" with "To begin with." While he did not follow "First" with "Second," he did keep his word choice parallel, a best practice to orient your audience, by repeating the word *here* in each of his transitions.

## TIP 14:  Link the parts of your speech to reinforce points.

Though your content is seared into your brain, it is new to the listeners in your audience, so remind them of your key points. Part 1 of Jock's speech focused on the friends of his blood, his family. In the last sentence of part 2 of his speech, notice how Jock subtly references family even though his attention has moved on to friends of his times:

> **(PART 2)**
> Now here, we have the friends of my times. Of school days and military service in good times and bad times. Of shared experience and common values. They are very important to me. But you would like them too because they think the way you do. They think, for example, that friends are the family you choose for yourself.

## TIP 15:  Prioritize your supporting points.

The order of your points should not be random. Since Jock spoke about an inspirational topic, he revealed his groups of friends in order of increasing emotional intensity. Prioritizing your points also allows you to allocate airtime. Jock appropriately devoted far more of the content in the body of his speech to his most important best friend, his wife, in part 3:

> **(PART 3)**
> And finally here, we have the friends of my heart. Of lovers. For me, that is my wife Robin. And I am lucky there too because I married a Toastmaster . . . and that is better thinking.

Now lovers are special kinds of friends because they are not imposed on us like family and school friends. Theirs is a friendship entered into gladly, willingly, joyfully, passionately. Sometimes in the springtime of life when young blood courses through vibrant veins, sometimes later in life when more sluggish blood cruises through varicose veins. My blood no longer courses, nor even cruises; it just coagulates.

But I can still savor the richness of life with my wife, my lover, my companion, my friend, for all my days. Because you see this friendship of lovers can last for the rest of our lives. Or it may burn with the power of a sunburst, hot and bright and brief to fade and die, leaving two burned-out husks bitter and twisted and scarred. Been there, done that, got the t-shirt.

Because sometimes love does fail. Without friendship, love cannot last. But with friendship, love can last forever. But like anything of value it must be earned and maintained, and we . . . we could all tell a thousand stories each. Nothing in themselves, but adding up together to something wonderful.

The two best practices for speech body construction are evident here in part 3. Jock used not only clear transitional words, "And finally here, we have the friends of my heart," but also strongly linked to his past friends, saying, "Now lovers are special kinds of friends because they are not imposed on us like family and school friends."

Unlike a personal audience, a business audience assumes points will be covered in descending order of importance, so start with your highest-priority content. Start with a trivial point, and you lose the interest of the decision makers in the room.

## TIP 16:  Tie up all loose ends.

Speeches do not have sequels, so tie up all loose ends. The dramatic principle known as "Chekhov's gun" demands, "If you say in the first chapter that there is a rifle hanging on the wall, in the second or third chapter it absolutely must go off." This principle also demands that the speaker eliminate any thread that cannot be tied up. Jock advises, "The primary thing is to know what you want to say. And so often, people do not. Instead, they fall in love with particular lines; I am as guilty as anybody of that. Often, a particular line or concept is not to the point—it is a diversion. You have to have the luxury of being able to walk away from your preparation and then come back to the speech cold and say: 'Yes, lovely as it is, I will keep this idea for the future because it is good, but it does not live in this speech.'"

Although Jock spoke of what he expected of his friends, he still needed to address what they could expect of him:

### (CONCLUSION)

So, what kind of a friend am I? Do my friends get from me what I get from them? I have never told them, never told them, the things I am telling you. But I do freely give them advice that they didn't ask for. I do give comfort when they need it. I do make them laugh when perhaps they would rather cry. I am always the same. I am always there. That's all I've got. But it's all theirs.

## TIP 17:  Call back to your introduction in your conclusion.

Speakers use callbacks, repetitions of words or phrases from a prior part of a speech, to kindle feelings of connectedness in an audience. Though callbacks are a technique often used by comedians at the end of a set to amplify humor by giving the audience the feeling of being in on the joke, this technique is equally effective when used at the end of a dramatic speech to amplify serious emotions. In Jock's conclusion, he called back to his "three o'clock in the morning" reference:

My friends, you, the friends of my times, have now met my three best friends. But you all have these same friends. Different names, different faces. But in some form or another, these are the people who will roll out of bed at three o'clock in the morning and come to your aid because you need them. And they know that you'd do the same for them.

Callbacks work even when they are indirect. David Nottage (1996) told a story in his introduction about struggling to learn how to ride a bicycle at age six. Mr. Nottage ended his speech with a reference to Olympic gymnast Kerri Strug (after injuring her left ankle on her first vault, Strug secured a gold medal for the U.S. team by courageously sticking the landing on her second vault) and called back to his opening story:

*She [Strug] had every right to stay down, but she got up. Mary Pickford said it best when she said, "This thing that we call failure. This thing that we call failure . . . It's not the falling down, it's the staying down." Ladies and gentlemen, how easy, how easy is it for us, you and I, to remember this simple secret for success? It should be as easy as falling off a bike.*

As a final example, consider Willie Jones's (1997) use of a sound as a callback. During his speech, he described helping his friends fix their computers by instructing them on how to reboot. He ended the first part of his speech with, "I can hear this sound that goes 'Boing!' and that lets me know that everything is fine. That sound is 'Boing!' Remember that." He closes the loop with his final words: "Just because you grow up, doesn't mean you have to grow old. Those of you who are baby boomers, let me hear you go, 'Boing!'"

### TIP 18: Summarize your key points and explicitly state your core message in your conclusion.

Audiences appreciate speakers who conclude by directly "telling them what you told them." While you need not recap everything, strive to summarize how the key points of your speech explicitly relate to your core message (or moral). Jock's core message was the value of friendship supported by his feelings toward the friends of his blood, times, and heart:

> Tomorrow, we shall all be gone from here, scattering to our homes across the world, but before we go, taking with us perhaps some new friendships. Let me just remind you that sitting next to you, right by your side, if you are lucky may be the friend of your heart, or of your times, or of your blood.

### TIP 19:  Issue a call to action in your conclusion.

Regardless of which general purpose a speech serves, it should influence what the members of an audience believe or how they act, preferably in a way that improves their lives or the lives of their loved ones. With his call to action to treasure and nurture the ties of friendship (along with another well-placed callback), Jock completed his championship speech:

> Reach out now in your minds and hearts and touch them.
> Feel their warmth. Feel their friendship. Feel the ties that bind.
> And if we treasure these ties, nurture these ties; then we'll have all the luck we'll ever need. And we won't need Facebook.
> Mr. Chairman.

### TIP 20:  Avoid the comparative framework, since it leaves your audience more confused.

Now that we have explored four of the six organizing frameworks covered in the Toastmasters *Competent Communication* manual, it's time to briefly turn our attention to the comparative framework that, as its name suggests, allows a speaker to compare the relative advantages and disadvantages of two or more alternatives.

Comparative speeches should be avoided, especially in business contexts, since they create uncertainty and complexity. Imagine you are a product marketer working for a cereal company and you have been asked to compare and contrast campaigns to increase sales either by issuing coupons to consumers or by discounting to grocery stores directly. You might argue that coupons are more expensive to distribute but are better at increasing your brand awareness. The problem is that using this approach is more likely to slow the decision-making process rather than accelerate it by comparing a variety of factors that are difficult to weigh against each other. This stands to reason because information is most valuable when it simply informs a decision. A comparative speech, even one with a recommendation, is too complex.

## TIP 21: Use the situation-complication-resolution framework for persuasive speeches.

The situation-complication-resolution framework is the best approach for crafting a persuasive speech because it uses storytelling to present a recommendation. To illustrate this, we must first transform the more familiar two-part problem-solution framework into the equivalent situation-complication-resolution framework.

In order to discuss any problem, you first need to provide an audience with the situation or context in which the problem arose. Next, share complications, or effects, resulting from an unanticipated change in the situation. By expanding "problem" into "situation-complication," the problem-solution approach becomes the more precise situation-complication-resolution framework.

Synonyms of *situation, complication,* and *resolution* can be substituted in any combination and still accomplish the same persuasive end. *Situation* can also mean *cause, circumstance, environment,* etc. *Complication* could be *effect, opportunity, issue,* and so on. *Resolution* may be framed as *solution, answer, recommendation,* etc. Stanford University professor and business communications expert Matt Abrahams makes it catchy with "What? So what? Now what?"

Our preferred framework is situation-complication-resolution because it uses terminology often applied to storytelling. In Act 1, you meet the hero in her ordinary world. This ordinary world establishes her physical and psychological situation before something casts her on a journey. Act 1 ends with an inciting incident that pits the hero against a formidable adversary. In Act 2, the hero must confront a series of increasingly intense trials. The business equivalents of these trials are the complications. Finally, Act 2 ends with an epic climax during which the hero prevails against all odds. In Act 3, the hero's journey comes to a resolution when she establishes a new, typically better, life.

A situation analysis is useful, even as a stand-alone presentation, since it demonstrates your ability to educate a decision maker. A situation-complication analysis is even better since it demonstrates your ability to brainstorm and to identify problems and their root causes. But using the situation-complication-resolution (aka problem-solution) analysis is best of all since the end result is a persuasive recommendation delivered on a silver platter. Stopping at the complication makes you a problem finder; providing the resolution makes you a more valuable and promotable problem solver.

Many employees fear that providing a strong recommendation is risky. As with most cases of trepidation, it is worth considering what is the worst that can happen. In our unscientific experience, our bosses have chosen our recommendations eight out of ten times. On the ninth time, they chose one of our ranked alternatives. And, yes, on the tenth time, they dismissed all our solutions and offered a clever approach that we had not considered. In no cases were we ever reprimanded or fired; in all cases we earned the respect of our managers as valuable, independent problem solvers.

## TIP 22:  Outline your speech to avoid memorization and reading.

Though many Toastmasters either read or memorize their first speech, neither technique is effective in a business setting. In both cases, you are likely to sound and look robotic or inauthentic. However, the bigger issue is that business presentations are often highly interactive. If you prioritize your written material over your message, then you will struggle to recover when you lose your place or if a question takes you in a different direction.

Start by writing your speech out word for word. This is important because it not only allows you to express your ideas, but also gives you a sense of how much time your speech is going to take. A typical rate of speech is 125 words per minute. Next, boil your speech down to an outline consisting of key points. Finally, rehearse it several times to internalize it and gain confidence. Yes, you will likely miss a point here or there. But remember that only you know what you forgot to say. As long as your general purpose and specific purpose are clear, you should consider your mission accomplished.

In most business settings you will present for a period of time and then take questions at the end. In this case, the approach just outlined is best. More frequently, you will be a facilitator rather than an orator and can dispense writing out your speech and just go straight to an outline. These days, such outlines get translated into presentation slides; however, the same ultimate objective remains. If you fully internalize your material, then you should eliminate the slides. The one exception, of course, is when you are presenting something highly technical where a picture truly is worth a thousand words.

• • • • •

Audiences are conditioned to expect three-part presentations with an introduction, body, and conclusion. Though by no means the only way to structure a persuasive presentation, the situation-complication-resolution framework will work for the vast majority of business pitches you make, and you will still have a great degree of flexibility in delivering the material. Business professionals who craft persuasive presentations position themselves more effectively for promotion than people who stick solely to sharing informational updates. The framework you choose serves as the skeleton of your speech. The better the skeleton, the more engaging the speech.

We have now covered all but one of the speech frameworks recommended by Toastmasters. The only framework we have not addressed—chronological—is the basis of classical storytelling, the format of choice for inspirational speeches and the focus of our next chapter.

## CHAPTER 3

# Telling Stories

## TIP 23:  Tell stories.

One of our favorite Native American proverbs sums up why we recommend that speakers include one or more stories in their speeches: "Tell me a fact, and I will learn. Tell me a truth, and I will believe. But tell me a story, and it will live in my heart forever."

While this proverb emerged from commonsense observation of which messages were sticky and which were not, neuroscience now answers why stories are effective as a conduit for learning. In an article in *Psychological Science*, researchers from Washington University in St. Louis concluded:

> *Different brain regions track different aspects of a story, such as a character's physical location or current goals. Some of these regions mirror those involved when people perform, imagine, or observe similar real-world activities. These results support the view that readers understand a story by simulating the events in the story world and updating their simulation when features of that world change.*[1]

As a speaker, it behooves you to tap into this direct feed into your audience's minds. Listeners actually experience the emotions and ideas embedded in stories by relating the stories to their own past experiences and forming new, synthetic experiences in the process.

This gift allows our civilization to learn to survive and thrive with zero risk and far less expenditure of time and physical energy.

## TIP 24:  Don't retell your story; relive your story.

Effective storytellers relive their stories on stage. The mantra "Don't retell your story; relive your story" is attributed to motivational speaker Lou Heckler and was popularized by Toastmasters world champion Craig Valentine (1999). In Craig's words, "You've got to invite them into the scene of your story so they can hear it how you heard it, see it how you saw it, and feel how you felt it." Retold stories feel backward-looking and clinical. Relived stories feel alive and emotional.

After shaking the emcee's hand and waiting for the applause to subside, Ed Tate (2000) began his speech with a four-second pause during which he made eye contact with the majority of his audience. Then, through another nine seconds of silence, he authoritatively stiffened his posture, withdrew a 3" × 5" top-opening memo pad from his inside coat pocket, flipped it open, tore off a page, and handed himself a speeding ticket. With his audience fully immersed in the scene, Ed began.

## One of Those Days (2000)

| Central message(s) | Compassion |
|---|---|
| Duration | 7.61 minutes |
| Words per minute | 143 |
| Laughs per minute | 4.86 |

**(INTRODUCTION)**

"There you go, Mr. Tate. Next time, drive a little slower."

Speaking of slow, have you ever wondered why it takes a police officer so long to write a ticket? Completely eliminating all that time that you have made up. I said to myself, "It's going to be one of those days."

---

Ed used silence to draw in his audience. He shared: "The vast majority of speakers start talking a nanosecond after they are introduced. Not me; I want to connect; I want to have that spiritual, emotional connection with the audience first. I know it sounds like woo-woo, but it's psychologically important to me."

Ed relived his story by bringing his characters to life on stage through voice and physical presence. When he embodied the police officer, he assumed an authoritative posture, constrained movement, and serious tone of voice. When he transitioned to being himself, Ed projected his natural expressiveness and personality. A speaker must be able to dial the level of theatricality up or down to suit the audience, as well as his own comfort level.

Ed also relived his story by employing realistic dialogue. Imagine if Ed had started with, "Running late, I was racing to the airport but got pulled over by the police. So frustrating!" While this passage has action and emotion, it does not engage the audience or set the scene in the way his character and internal dialogue did.

Real dialogue quickly conveys emotion. It achieves verisimilitude by bending the rules of formal writing with contractions, partial sentences, and even the occasional "um," "like," or "you know." Think about how we converse with our friends. Though dialogue can be used (very sparingly) to share information, its primary purpose is either to move the story forward or to contribute to revealing a character's strengths, flaws, and desires.

Real dialogue is most powerful when it conveys the subtext, or deeper meaning, of a character's true emotions and desires. The mantra of good storytelling—"show; don't tell"—applies to writing dialogue. If dialogue explicitly tells what a character is thinking, doing, or feeling, then it is not realistic. In an effort to protect their egos from humiliation, characters are at the very least vague and often make statements that are contradictory to what they actually want. In addition to beating around the bush and lying, the other common form of subtext-laden dialogue involves characters discussing a topic that serves as a symbolic or metaphorical representation of a looming, unspoken issue.

Within reason, each character should have a distinct speech pattern or voice. Drawing on stereotypes, younger characters might speak more slowly and with less-than-crisp enunciation. When the speaker is a woman, she might adopt a lower pitch when delivering male dialogue. An older character may be portrayed with a slightly gruffer voice. Sometimes using a regional accent is appropriate. When delivering most dialogue, each character's voice needs only to be tailored enough to be distinct. The exception, of course, is for over-the-top characters used for comic relief.

## TIP 25: Create a protagonist with strengths, weaknesses, and goals.

Even if you have great plot, your speech needs characters that fit squarely into the archetypical roles listeners expect to encounter. Adhering to conventional character types amplifies emotional impact. The audience naturally yearns for the hero to succeed and hates the villain for getting in the hero's way. Moreover, these archetypes are critical time savers.

As Ed continued his story, he revealed his strengths, weaknesses, and goals.

### (PART 1)

But I did the math, and there was still time for me to make the noon flight to Phoenix, Arizona. All I had to do was park my car, go through Security and off to the gate. As luck would have it,

I found a parking spot right away. But when I made it to Security, there were lines as far as the eye could see. For the first time in aviation history, United had decided to enforce the two-bag limit. I did the math. There was no way I was going to make my noon flight. It's going to be one of those days.

Now I was upset with United. It was because of their policy that I was going to miss my flight. At least that was going to be my story. I looked on the departure board. There was a two o'clock flight to Phoenix. If I made that flight, I could still make my meeting. I said to myself, "I'm a frequent flyer with United. I've paid tens of thousands of dollars with this airline. They had better figure out a way to get me on that plane; otherwise I'm going to give them a piece of my mind."

The primary role in every story belongs to the protagonist, so always introduce the hero at the beginning of your story. Ed, along with an overwhelming majority of Toastmasters champions, used the first-person perspective, which means he played the role of the protagonist.

There is one great danger in telling personal stories: putting yourself on a pedestal. This can happen in many subtle and not-so-subtle ways. Many amateur speakers share their bona fides in a heavy-handed way, for example, by rattling off their impressive biography at the start of their talk. Ed's strengths—his travel savvy and frequent flier status—were important to the story yet subtle.

There are less obvious and often unintentional ways, though, for a speaker to raise himself above an audience. In an honest desire to appear authoritative and confident, some speakers mistakenly share only their successes. By choosing not to reveal vulnerability, they lose an important way to bond with the audience and generate empathy. Ed avoided this error early in his speech by revealing the basic human frailties of procrastination and hubris.

Well-developed protagonists have multiple goals or needs. Typically, the protagonist has an extrinsic goal that he knows and an intrinsic goal that he is not aware of but that is clear to his audience.

Ed's extrinsic goal is getting on a flight to Phoenix. Most often, the protagonist's intrinsic need is to overcome a character flaw that either allows him to obtain his extrinsic goal or redirects him to an even better outcome. Though we are not far enough along in the story to know for certain, we suspect that he must have an epiphany in the story's climax about one or both of his frailties.

## TIP 26: Challenge your protagonist with a worthy opponent.

### (PART 2)

I made it over to Customer Service. In front of me there was a couple. A tall young man and his girlfriend. The conversation between the tall young man and the [female] Customer Service agent went something like this: "What do you mean there's no room for us on the two o'clock flight to Phoenix? It's because of United Airlines I missed our connection in the first place. I'm a frequent flyer. I've spent tens of thousands of dollars on this airline. You had better figure out a way to get us on that plane."

The Customer Service agent said, "Sir, the next flight where I can get both of you on the flight is at six o'clock."

He said, "Do the math, lady. The wedding is at five." Then he committed the unpardonable sin. He called her the B word and the silence was deafening. Then he stormed off and I was next. Oh boy, it's going to be one of those days.

Well-developed protagonists are enough to make a good story. But to make a great story, there must be an opponent, introduced early on, worthy of doing battle with the protagonist.

The most believable stories have opponents who are larger than life, yet equally matched with the protagonist. If your opponent is a pushover, your story will be short and boring. If your opponent is completely invincible, your audience will not believe it when your protagonist defeats him. Spend as much time crafting your villain as you do your protagonist. Typically, the villain either shares the same extrinsic goal as the protagonist or has a goal that, if achieved, prevents the hero from obtaining his goal.

Ed's character web is very sophisticated. Who is the opponent in Ed's story? Is it the police officer who wrote him a ticket and who might reappear? Is it United Airlines and its customer service agent? Is it the establishment, a combination of the police and the airline? Is it the tall, angry, rude young man?

In a simple story, character development begins with a protagonist and an opponent. More textured stories add allies and enemies along the journey. The most textured stories add subtle characters, including false allies and false enemies that temporarily mislead the audience. The police officer was a standard enemy, introduced uncharacteristically early; he will not reappear. United Airlines and the customer service agent are false enemies, first standing in Ed's way and later coming to his aid. Like the police officer, the angry young man is a standard enemy.

The villains in winning Toastmasters speeches have almost always been intangible evils. These evils are the foil to the core message. When the speech inspires people to persevere, the intangible evil is fear. For action, it is complacency. For love and compassion, it is intolerance, discrimination, or simply rudeness. As we discover by the end of his story, Ed's speech is *no* exception to the "intangible evil" norm. Because audiences and judges expect to be inspired, the opponent must always be defeated in the end. There is no sequel.

### TIP 27: Introduce a mentor to humanize and arm the protagonist.

I made eye contact with the Customer Service agent, and all of a sudden it occurred to me that she was trying to do the best that she could. She was trying to provide for her family just like me. I was no better than her. I made eye contact with her, and I said, "Ma'am, take your time. I'm in no hurry." Not anymore.

> She said, "Sir, what can I do for you today?"
>
> I said, "Ma'am, I couldn't help but overhear that the next flight to Phoenix is booked. If you can put me on any flight to Phoenix today, that would be fine." Her fingers danced across the keyboard, and she presented me with a ticket on the two o'clock flight to Phoenix. "Hallelujah, hallelujah!" I really didn't do that, but it was close. I said, "Ma'am, thank you very much, and don't let it be one of those days."

Some speakers put themselves on a pedestal by telling stories where they make it through an epic struggle all on their own. That might sound admirable, but audience members can only connect if they believe they can achieve the same success the speaker achieved. To make that connection, the speaker must not appear to be special but should persevere with a special process, a highly effective approach for overcoming obstacles, which is revealed to the audience as the story progresses. There is nothing special about Ed; rather, he uses the special process of kindness and compassion toward others to get to Phoenix on time.

The speaker can develop this special process on her own or obtain it from a mentor. Though both approaches are effective, the mentor approach is almost always better. By discovering a special recipe for success independently, a speaker seems smarter than and superior to the audience, but learning from a wise mentor puts the speaker eye to eye, heart to heart with the audience. Just as the speaker gained a valuable gift from someone else, the speaker pays that gift forward to the audience.

The customer service agent in Ed's story is not an ordinary false enemy who transforms into a standard ally. She turns into a full-fledged mentor who not only rewards Ed's kindness with his extrinsic goal, a ticket to get to Phoenix in time for his meeting, but also gives him his first taste of what it means to pay kindness forward.

Mentors come in all forms in winning Toastmasters speeches. Mostly, they are family members and friends. However, there have been unusual mentors, such as inanimate objects. Ed Hearn (2006) learned how to bounce back from a bowl-shaped weight he extracted from a child's inflatable punching bag. Another clever example was Willie Jones's (1997) mentor, a computer that taught him how to press Control-Alt-Delete on his past regrets.

The most unusual mentors are intangible. Dwayne Smith (2002) shared a touching story about how music instilled lifesaving hope when his friend was at the brink of suicide. Mark Brown (1995) used a cartoon character from Disney's *Beauty and the Beast* to dramatize intolerance. And in a moment of creative brilliance, Craig Valentine (1999) brought his own reflection to life to teach himself the benefit of mindfulness enabled by silence.

Though now considered clichéd, it was not uncommon for speakers in the past to build stories using major historical figures as mentors. Brett Rutledge (1998) referenced John F. Kennedy, Martin Luther King Jr., and Albert Einstein as examples of people who ignored the establishment and dared to dream. Darren LaCroix (2001) drew inspiration from rocketry pioneer Robert Goddard to show what people can achieve if they refuse to give up.

In stories, mentors often boost audience appeal. Excluding historical figures, in nearly every winning Toastmasters speech between 1995 and 2012 that had a human mentor, the mentor was female.

### TIP 28:  Craft a high-stakes climax.

**(PART 3)**

I had some time to kill, so I decided to go over to the food court, and who was in line ahead of me? The tall, angry young man and his girlfriend. I said to myself, "Boy, I hope they get his order right."

I also thought to myself, "You know someone ought to say something to that guy. Someone ought to give him a piece of their mind. Someone ought to do that. Then I heard this voice, and it said, "Ed, if not you, then who?" I hate when this happens.

I started to walk towards them; by the way, did I mention that he was tall? Six foot four, about 220. Folks, don't let the video screens fool you. I am not a big man. I tapped him on the shoulder. I said, "Excuse me, sir, I know it's none of my business, but if it's true what you say and you are a frequent flyer, then you know two things. Number one, the question is not if, the question is when you will miss your next flight. And number two, the Customer Service agent, she's not a pilot. She had nothing to do with you missing your connection, but next time this happens, and it will happen again, I want you to be nice."

Then all of a sudden—POW! [*long dramatic pause*]—his girl-friend hit him in the arm and said, "Yeah, be nice." Now some of you all thought I got hit, didn't you? He walked away in stunned silence rubbing his arm.

At the beginning of this chapter we highlighted research proving that listeners vicariously share the experiences of the storyteller. In the climax of a story, when the stakes are highest for the protagonist, the stakes are also highest for the audience. The more life-or-death the climax, the more the audience is engaged and believes that a pro-tagonist has earned his reward. Earlier, in the customer service line, Ed had his first taste of the power of compassion, a virtue with the ability to neutralize hubris, his tragic flaw. However, Ed needed to demonstrate a selfless ability to stand up for others in a high-stakes situation to complete his transformation. Confronting the angry young man at the food court put Ed in real danger. When Ed said, "Then all of a sudden—POW!" his audience was certain the angry young man had hit Ed.

## TIP 29:  Tell your audience the moral of the story.

### (CONCLUSION)

Finally, I made it to the gate and I noticed something unusual. Typically a gate is manned by uniformed personnel, but on this particular occasion in addition to them there was a man in a suit. Usually suits mean trouble, and I thought to myself, maybe that Customer Service rep wasn't supposed to give me this ticket.

I handed my ticket to the gate agent, and the gate agent whispers to the suit, "This is the guy."

I said, "Oh no, they're going to take my ticket."

The gentleman in the suit said, "Mr. Tate, I'm the General Manager for United Airlines. I want to thank you for what you have done."

As I reached up to shake his hand, I said, "He's just trying to soften me up so he can take my ticket." I said, "What am I being thanked for?"

He said, "Sir, one of our supervisors was at the food court, and she witnessed when you confronted the angry young man. You see, Mr. Tate, our number one priority is to get our passengers safely to their destination, and we do that every single day. Occasionally we get them there on time. Seldom, if ever, does anyone stand up for us, and I just want to thank you sir. Mr. Tate, may I please have your ticket."

Darn it, I knew it. He was going to take my ticket, but the gate agent handed me a first-class ticket on the two o'clock flight to Phoenix, and it was like I always said, I knew it was going to be one of those days. Mr. Toastmaster.

Speakers are obliged to tell the moral of the story. It is perfectly acceptable and effective to deliver the moral overtly, as most do. Ed could have said, "That day, I realized I had been leading a selfish life. So often, we see something and only say something if it affects us personally. I learned that I have a moral obligation to stand up for others even if they will never know and even if it comes at a cost to me." By embedding his moral in the dialogue of the general manager, Ed's approach was subtle yet equally effective. It is also very much in keeping with his style: "I do not preach. I share lessons from my life, but I leave the choice of applying those lessons up to each listener."

## TIP 30:   Tell stories using a three-act hero's journey structure.

Now that we have experienced Ed Tate's entire speech piece by piece, let's reassemble it to see how he applied the classic hero's journey structure. Though there is no official definition, modern storytelling experts such as Joseph Campbell, Christopher Vogler, and Robert McKee provide some insight on what a complete, three-act story looks like.

Act 1 introduces the protagonist in his ordinary world. We get to know the essential details of his abilities, his mindset, his desires, his relationships, and his flaws. At the end of Act 1, the hero experiences an inciting incident that casts him on a journey.

Act 2 subjects the protagonist to a series of escalating intrapersonal, interpersonal, or extrapersonal (e.g., societal) conflicts. Emerging from each trial, the protagonist accumulates tools and knowledge that he will need to defeat his opponent in the explosive climax at the end of the act.

Act 3 ties loose ends, and we see the protagonist at home in his new world, transformed physically, morally, or, more often, emotionally.

Today we may be more familiar with the "Pixar pitch" espoused by Matthew Luhn, head of story at the acclaimed animation studio. Here is an overlay of that technique on the three-act narrative structure. The ordinary world in Act 1 maps to "Once upon a time . . . And every day . . ." The next part, "Until one day . . . ," is the inciting incident that bridges Act 1 to Act 2. The progressive complications of Act 2 are Pixar's "And because of that . . . And because of that . . . And because of that . . ." The climax begins with "Until finally . . ." The story then concludes with the new normal world and the illumination of the core message, "And after that . . . And the moral of the story is . . ."

Using the Pixar pitch, let's deconstruct Ed's story. Once upon a time, Ed was a seasoned business traveler with a stereotypical sense of entitlement. Until one day, he was stopped for speeding on the way to the airport and missed his flight. And because of that, he waited in the customer service line behind another, similarly entitled, traveler who verbally abused the ticketing agent . . . and because of that he showed compassion to the agent, who rewarded him with the desired seat. Until finally, Ed confronted the other traveler in the food court, demanding that he treat others with respect. And after that, Ed was further rewarded with an upgrade to first class. And the moral of the story is: Be compassionate and stand up for others even if they will never know and even if it comes at a cost.

## TIP 31:  Bring your audience into your setting.

Perhaps the biggest mistake is being too vague about the setting. Consider the following lines from a Toastmaster who came to us looking for help with her speech (some details changed to protect the innocent):

> Years ago, when I first started to work for the University of Rhodesia as an International Student Advisor, there were only two employees operating the International Student Office. Every day, I just put my head down and focused on getting the job done. I noticed that my coworker Jane would go into our boss's office at least once a day to discuss a variety of things, both work-related and personal.

To be realistic, to allow the audience to relive the story, the setting must be specific in time, location, and atmosphere. In the example above, the speaker is imprecise about time in two ways. First, by using "Years ago," the audience members do not know if it was 2 years, 5 years, or 10 years. Consequently, they cannot turn the clock back to put themselves at the right point in historical time. Second, by beginning the second sentence with "Every day," the audience cannot picture an exact day. The whole setup is fuzzy.

The speaker did a better job of describing the location—the International Student Office at the University of Rhodesia. But audiences need sensory description to re-create the scene. Could she hear the sound of students speaking a babel of languages? Could she smell and even taste the chalk dust lingering in the air? Could she feel the smoothness of her worn wooden chair arm? Though all these details need not and should not be provided all at once, the speaker could have offered a few more particulars to bring the people in her audience into her office so that they could emotionally feel what she felt.

Atmosphere, the final element of setting, is the key to establishing the mood. Perhaps this example could have been set during the long, slow days of summer recess when Jane had nothing better to do than brownnose with the boss in his air-conditioned, fluorescent-lit office. Just describing the season, weather, lighting, and even physical objects conveys mood and helps the speaker establish the setting with fewer words. Each of Ed Tate's settings—the side of the road during a traffic stop, the airport security line "as far as the eye could see," the airport customer service line, the food court, and the airline gate—triggers specific emotions. Bring the people in your audience into your setting by guiding them to where you want them to go but allow them to use their own imagination to fill in the scene.

## TIP 32: Build a logical narrative structure by choosing the variety and progression of stories.

So far, you have seen two of the most common ways to develop speeches. Jock Elliott's (2011) speech, in Chapter 2, consisted of an introduction, a body with three points, and a conclusion. Ed Tate's speech, in this chapter, tells the story of a hero's journey in chronological order. However, although there are endless opportunities to creatively build the narrative structure for any speech, it is very important to keep a consistent theme throughout and to utilize your title to reinforce your message.

Looking back on the 17-year period between 1995 and 2011, we found that 14 speakers won the world championship with speeches that comprised *several* stories. During that time period, winners told a single story three times, two stories four times, three stories seven times, and four stories three times. While the rule of three dominates, there is no hard-and-fast rule about the quantity of stories.

In addition to story variety, the other element needed for building a strong narrative is story progression, which is simply the chronological flow of a story or sequence of stories. The four types of story progression include linear, independent, flashback, and nonlinear.

In a linear progression, a speaker tells her stories in standard chronological order. Past world champions delivered their speeches using a strict linear progression six times between 1995 and 2011.

The independent story progression, where the speaker tells multiple stories that have no obvious chronological progression, was equally common, with six instances. Independent stories must share the speech's central message as a theme but need not share any core elements such as characters or setting.

By way of illustration, consider the independent narrative structure of Mark Brown's speech (1995). Mark leads off with the aphorism "We never get a second chance to make a first impression." The body of his speech has two independent stories, one less than is typical of the usual speech, so Mark was able to provide significantly more detail in his remaining stories. In the first, he recounts the plot elements of Disney's *Beauty and the Beast* to illustrate that intolerance, ignorance, and indifference are alive and well in the world of fantasy. In his second story, Mr. Brown described how NBC television news anchor Pat Harper spent five days living as a homeless person on the icy streets of New York City in January 1995. Though independent with respect to characters, setting, time, and even reality, these stories highlighted that intolerance, ignorance, and indifference were alive and well in the real world. Mark concluded his speech by asking the audience members to look at themselves in the mirror so that they would henceforth remember to give others a second chance.

This book's coauthor, Ryan Avery (2012), used a flashback story progression. This progression is a variation on the linear theme and was previously used by Vikas Jhingran (2007) and by David Henderson (2010). In the introduction to "Trust Is a Must," Ryan dangled a decision that would change his life forever: "Ryan, do you promise [to marry] me?" The audience was left at this Act 1 cliff-hanger with the words "Before I make my commitment . . ." Ryan transitioned into the body of his speech and linearly progressed through a three-story flashback. Finally, he returned to the altar at the end of his speech and answered, "Chelsea, I promise."

David Henderson's speech is a noteworthy variation on the flash-back progression. Whereas Ryan started his story, turned the clock back, and then returned chronologically, David used an embedded flashback purely for character development. David's story begins as he and his childhood best friend Jackie Parker are pretending to be fighter pilots trying to defeat the Red Baron, the decorated World War I German fighter pilot and Snoopy's nemesis. The body of David's speech begins with a flashback designed to reveal the emotional bond formed when he met Jackie at a kindergarten Halloween costume contest. Note that there was no inciting incident at the end of the introductory fighter pilot vignette. David simply reversed the chronological order of two pieces that establish the ordinary world in Act 1 of his story. David's speech transitions into Act 2 by returning to the end of the fighter pilot scene when Jackie falls down, recovers too slowly, and is diagnosed with sickle-cell anemia. Sadly, Jackie passes away at the climax of Act 2. In Act 3, David is transformed to his new normal when he overcomes his fear of death and accepts that losing people is part of loving people.

Though several world champions—especially in earlier years—blended linear and independent stories, only one successfully claimed victory with the nonlinear progression. This approach is artful but carries the risk of appearing chaotic. In addition, it is also extremely challenging for the storyteller to keep straight in his mind. We can readily think of two cinematic examples that illustrate the nonlinear approach: One is the reverse chronology of Christopher Nolan's 2000 film *Memento*. A more complex version is Quentin Tarantino's 1994 story weave in *Pulp Fiction*.

The 2001 Toastmasters champion, Darren LaCroix, was victorious with Tarantino's method. He began his speech by acting out a dramatic statement of a common problem that people face—we give up too quickly when confronted with adversity. He supported this assertion with Act 1 of his first story when he went into debt after buying a Subway sandwich shop. Next, he delivered Act 1 of his second story about rocket pioneer Robert Goddard. And next he shared Act 1 of his third story, a personal vignette about his desire to become a comedian. Then he successively delivered Act 2 of the Goddard story, Act 2 and Act 3 of the comedian story, Act 2 and Act 3 of the Subway story, and then Act 3 of the Goddard story. To recap, that weave is story 1, 2, 3, 2, 3, 3, 1, 1, 2. Finally, he concluded by asking his audience to take the next step, demonstrating that you can still make progress even when you fail. Though his nonlinear progression was extremely complex, or perhaps because of it, he delivered what is widely regarded to be one of the best Toastmasters speeches of all time.

## TIP 33: Adjust the technical depth to your message and your audience.

Ed Tate missed his flight due to poor planning on his part and a rule change on the part of United Airlines. However, the availability of seats on the next flight out falls into the extremely technical domain of flight capacity planning and scheduling. Airlines use highly sophisticated, real-time probabilistic models that optimize profit based on tens if not hundreds of factors accounting for passenger demand, weather, flight crews, and equipment.[2] Yet Ed wisely mentioned none of this since his inspirational message was about compassion and his audience neither knew nor needed to know about the mathematical intricacies of flight operations.

Speakers must adjust the technical depth to their message and their audience. If Ed were a transportation scientist addressing peers at an industry conference, it would have been perfectly appropriate for him to tread into deep technical waters.

Even in work environments that demand extremely technical presentations, you risk losing an audience if you share overly challenging material. Remember, the point of a presentation is not to dazzle an audience with your brilliance but to inform, inspire, persuade, or entertain for the benefit of your audience. Strive to make your material simple, but not simplistic, by starting at a high level and progressively peeling the onion to reveal layers of increasing technical depth. Share your expertise and your passion with your listeners, viewing them as respected peers and not as ignoramuses to be schooled or lectured.

While world champions generally avoid explaining technical subject matter because it takes time away from storytelling, a few examples exist. David Henderson explained the following during his speech:

> Many of you are wondering the same thing I wondered. What's sickle cell? It's a genetic blood disorder. People think of it as an African American disease, but it affects people all over the world, from the Middle East to Asia to South America. People with sickle cell have deformed red blood cells, which carry oxygen through your blood vessels. Normal cells look like disks and pass freely through your blood vessels. Sickle cells look like sickles. They clump together causing traffic jams, which in turn cause episodes. First you're fine, and then you get an infection, and then you're fine, and then you're in pain, and then you're fine, and then you die. There is no known cure.

From prior practice, David likely knew that many of his audience members would know neither the nature nor the expected outcome of a disease that afflicted one of the principal characters in his story. Technical explanations are risky, but there are several best practices that make them safer. First and foremost, practice your explanation in front of diverse audiences to ensure it is concise and clear. Toastmasters can do this in clubs all over their district, and business professionals can practice with coworkers or as a guest at a Toastmasters club. Second, consider using an accessible visual metaphor as David did in referring to "traffic jams." Third, add emotional depth to the explanation. David did this by showing the disease was universal. In addition, the phrase "and then you die" created tension by foreshadowing the passing of his best friend.

Though David did not do so in his explanation of sickle-cell anemia, speakers occasionally reference large numbers to transform statistics from the logical to the emotional. The traffic jam metaphor was most effective because it described something that causes daily pain to almost every individual in the audience.

Another common tactic for making numbers emotionally resonant is to simultaneously reference their scale at the global and personal level. For example, David could have said, "The Centers for Disease Control and Prevention estimates that sickle-cell disease affects 100,000 Americans. This means about 1 in 3,000 Americans will suffer medical complications and have shorter lives as a result of the disease. For African Americans, the number jumps to 1 in 500."[3]

## TIP 34: Eliminate jargon.

Most of the time, technical jargon, especially acronyms and industry slang, should be eliminated from your presentations. Do not fall into the trap of thinking that using such language positions you as an expert. Realistically, you run a much greater risk of coming off as less professional by making your content overly dense. In addition, you will lose that portion of your audience that is not as well versed in the meaning of the jargon you are slinging.

However, there may be occasions when jargon, used sparingly, can be valuable. For example, imagine that you are speaking to scuba-diving industry experts at their annual conference and need to feel that you are one of them. If you laboriously said "Professional Association of Diving Instructors" instead of the familiar "PADI," they would instantly recognize you as an outsider. In this instance, the entire audience is intimately familiar with the acronym, so it is the correct choice for building credibility.

## TIP 35: Choose messages with universal audience appeal.

David Henderson, the 2010 world champion, advises speakers to be mindful by choosing stories that appeal to both men and women. Men, in Toastmasters speeches and especially in business presentations, are particularly guilty of using sports and war metaphors, something female listeners might not always relate to as strongly.

●　　●　　●　　●　　●

When sharing a story, make sure to pick a topic about which you have both knowledge and passion. With a theme as the backbone, effective stories are fleshed out with plot, character, dialogue, and setting. To add richness, you need to layer on humor, which we turn to as the focus of the next chapter.

## CHAPTER 4

# Using Humor

**TIP 36:** **Get your first laugh fast to release tension, build rapport, and prime your audience to like you and be open to your message.**

At the beginning of a speech, just as the applause melts away, the audience falls into silence and stillness. This change introduces physical and psychological tension in the room. Out of respect, people with a tickle in their throat hold back their cough; people who are uncomfortable in their chair wait to shift their weight. This tension is precisely why getting the first laugh fast is so critical to building a connection with the audience. The audience wants the speaker—no, *needs* the speaker—to release the pressure valve in the room with humor. Speakers who melt tension are rewarded with likability, the basis of rapport.

Before winning the World Championship of Public Speaking, Darren LaCroix (2001) was a stand-up comic. Consequently, it should come as no surprise that his speech was among the funniest in the history of the contest. He secured his first laugh in just 21 seconds by falling facedown on the stage. Darren's objective was not only to get a laugh but also to prime his audience to receive his message: "When I fell on my face at the 22 clubs I practiced at, everyone said, 'Get up sooner; I was uncomfortable.' My coach Mark Brown said, 'Stay down longer; they are uncomfortable. Darren, our job as speakers is not to make people feel comfortable; it is to incite change.'"

For normal speakers, getting a large audience to laugh in less than half a minute is a major accomplishment. But in the World Championship of Public Speaking, seconds matter. From 1995 to 2011, the champions earned their first laugh after an average of just 25 seconds. The slowest was Jock Elliott (2011) at 88 seconds. The fastest during that time period was Brett Rutledge in 1998, who got his first laugh in just 4 seconds with "I was the kind of kid your parents told you to not play with."

Before we delve more deeply into humor, read Darren's complete speech within which we have indicated and numbered each laugh he garnered.

# Ouch! (2001)

| Central message(s) | Perseverance |
|---|---|
| Duration | 7.88 minutes |
| Words per minute | 124 |
| Laughs per minute | 3.68 |

### (INTRODUCTION)

Can you remember a moment when a brilliant idea flashed into your head? It was perfect for you. And then all of a sudden from the depths of your brain, another thought started forcing its way forward through the enthusiasm until finally it shouted, "Yeah, great idea, but what if you [*Laugh #1*] fall on your face?" [*Laugh #2*]

What do you do when you fall on your face? Do you try and jump right up and hope no one noticed? [*Laugh #3*] Are you more concerned with what other people will think than what you can learn from this? [*Laugh #4*]

Mr. Contest Chair [*Laugh #5*], friends, and the people way in the back, ouch! [*Laugh #6*] Did you feel I stayed down too long? [*Laugh #7*] Have you ever stayed down too long?

## (PART 1)

After four years of business school I went out and I went for the American dream. I bought a Subway sandwich shop. [*Laugh #8*] Oh, yeah. You're all impressed, I can tell. [*Laugh #9*] I don't want to brag or anything, but in six short months I took a $60,000 debt and I doubled that debt. [*Laugh #10*] That's right. I turned a Subway sandwich shop into a nonprofit organization. [*Laugh #11*] I financially fell on my face.

## (PART 2)

But then I remembered I was not the only one from my hometown of Auburn to fall on his face. You see, a hundred years earlier my childhood hero, Dr. Robert Goddard, had a ridiculous idea about building a device to take off from the ground and reach the stars. Dr. Goddard was the reason we landed on the moon.

## (PART 3)

I remember when I had my ridiculous idea. I was listening to a tape of Brian Tracy, a great speaker. He asked the question. He said, "What would you dare to dream if you knew you wouldn't fail?"

I struggled for an answer and then . . . Bing! I'd be a comedian. [*Laugh #12*] But you have to understand my background. I wasn't funny. [*Laugh #13*] I wasn't considered a class clown. In fact, the first time my brother ever laughed at me was when I told him I wanted to be a comedian. [*Laugh #14*] Ouch! [*Laugh #15*]

Who do you want to be? What changes do you want to make in your life? So many of us can see clearly where we want to go, and yet we go back and forth. If I just had a little more time. If I just had a little more money. If the kids were just a little older, but we never take that first step.

**(PART 4)**

Dr. Goddard's first flight took off in Auburn and landed . . . in Auburn. [*Laugh #16*] It only reached 41 feet, but it was a first step.

There are strangers out there, people that don't even know you who will make fun of your first step. When the local press found out about Dr. Goddard's ridiculous idea to reach the moon and his first flight, the next morning the headlines read, "Moon Rocket Misses Target by 238,799-and-a-Half Miles." [*Laugh #17*] Ouch! [*Laugh #18*] But those strangers are part of your process.

**(PART 5)**

We also have friends and family that love us and don't want to see us fall on our face. Imagine my parents' reaction when after stretching their budget to help me through college, seeing me fall on my face, and then I come home, "Mom, Dad, I want to be a comedian." [*Laugh #19*] I was met by silence. [*Laugh #20*] They too are part of your process.

**(PART 6)**

After a year of struggling in the comedy world, I'll never forget one night. I was bombing for 20 minutes. It was horrible. [*Laugh #21*] So, I went for my surefire bit. I brought a woman up from the audience, and she stood directly behind me. She put her hands forward in place of mine. It's an old improv technique. She would tell the story with her hand gestures as I would tell it verbally, and it works best the more animated the hands are. This woman stood there like an ancient statue. [*Laugh #22*] She didn't move. I turned to her in desperation. I said, "Please do something with your hands." [*Laugh #23*] She did [*covers mouth*]. [*Laugh #24*] Ouch! [*Laugh #25*]

I immediately called my mentor, Rick. I said, "Rick, I bombed. I think I died. They hated me."

Rick said, "So?"

"What do you mean so?" [*Laugh #26*] How do you argue with *so*?

And then Rick reminded me every comedian, every speaker, anyone who has accomplished anything has fallen on their face. It's part of your process.

### (PART 7)

And then I remembered Subway. I fell on my face, but I never took the next step. It's the step after the ouch that's so important. It's so difficult. We don't like the ouch. We don't want to take that step, but when that foot lands, you are going to like that feeling. We learn from the ouch.

### (PART 8)

In an effort to reach the moon, Dr. Goddard said, "Failures, I consider valuable negative information. Information essential to each step getting closer to the moon." Dr. Goddard was an ouch master. [*Laugh #27*] We need to be ouch masters.

### (CONCLUSION)

If you're willing to fail, you can learn anything. I still have my day job, but now in my hometown in a comedy club my picture hangs on the wall, but it's because I took the step after the ouch.

I wasn't given the gift of making people laugh. I was given the opportunity to take a next step. So were you. What's your next step? When will you take it? Take it.

I didn't want to look back on my life and think, "Never did try that comedy thing, but instead I paid all my bills." [*Laugh #28*] We're all going to move forward and try and reach a point, but we're going to reach a point headed to our goals where we get stuck and we can't move. If we're always so afraid of that ouch, we forget that if we lean forward and take a risk and fall on our face, we still made progress. [*Laugh #29*] Go ahead and fall. Fall forward.

## TIP 37:  Use humor in every speech.

Why is humor so important in public speaking? After all, there was no humor in Abraham Lincoln's 1863 "Gettysburg Address" or Martin Luther King Jr.'s 1963 "I Have a Dream" speech. However, these and other speeches deemed to be the greatest of all time were designed to galvanize, educate, grieve, and inspire hope for a brighter tomorrow. Mostly political, these speeches were crafted to change the destiny of the world.

Until very recently, comic relief was neither expected nor accepted in great oratory, especially during moments of national mourning. However, it is instructive to compare President Reagan's address to the American people following the space shuttle *Challenger* disaster with that of President Obama following a mass shooting at Sandy Hook Elementary School.

Following the loss of seven astronauts, President Reagan addressed the American citizens with a eulogy that is considered another of the great speeches in modern American rhetoric. He put space exploration in context as a risky but worthy endeavor that must continue to be pursued. He respectfully acknowledged the grief of the astronauts' families, of the many children who watched the shuttle disintegrate on live television, and of the employees of NASA. His 650-word speech was filled with strong emotion. Hope and perseverance, rather than humor, were the relief valves.

On December 14, 2012, 20 young children and 6 adults were tragically and seemingly randomly killed at Sandy Hook Elementary School by a heavily armed gunman. President Obama addressed the families, the citizens of Newtown, Connecticut, and the American nation two days later. He offered heartfelt condolences and issued a promise to reform America's lax gun-control standards. About a quarter of the way into his 1,670-word speech, President Obama allowed listeners to release their pain a little with the following story:

*And then there were the scenes of the schoolchildren, helping one another, holding each other, dutifully following instructions in the way that young children sometimes do; one child even trying to encourage a grown-up by saying, "I know karate. So it's okay. I'll lead the way out."*

Even in tragedy, we begin the process of healing with laughter. The laughter that people expressed upon hearing this story was the laughter of release.

In venues outside politics and social reform, and especially in Toastmasters contests, the speaker's purpose is to inspire and to entertain. Humor serves both purposes. Inspiration stirs deep emotions, and humor is the sugar that helps the medicine go down. It's a foundational pillar of entertainment.

### TIP 38: Crank up the laughs per minute with a sense of superiority, surprise, or release.

In the 17 years between 1995 and 2011, world champions averaged an impressive 2.5 laughs per minute. Even the least humorous winner, Mark Brown in 1995, averaged just over one joke per minute. The second-lowest was Dwayne Smith in 2002, who averaged 1.4 laughs per minute. During the course of his 7-minute, 52-second speech, Darren LaCroix, whose speech you read above, elicited laughter from the audience 29 times. This worked out to approximately 3.7 laughs per minute.[1]

In order to understand how to get the most laughs per minute, we must first delve into the psychology of laughter. At present, there is no grand unified theory of why people laugh. Instead, there are three explanations that are complementary and overlapping.

The first theory of why humans laugh is to claim superiority. A great deal of humor falls squarely into this category, including laughing at people who make bad decisions or are eccentric. This type of humor is amplified when the person is in a position of authority and fits a particular stereotype—politically correct or not. Superiority-based humor has an escalating scale of viciousness, starting with gentle parody and satire, moving to moderate sarcasm, and progressing to scathing insults.

Darren got a series of laughs because he allowed his audience to feel superior at his expense, a sentiment known as schadenfreude. With fair warning that deconstructing humor destroys it, consider how Darren described his first entrepreneurial venture, "I don't want to brag or anything, but in six short months I took a $60,000 debt and I doubled that debt. [*Laugh #10*] That's right. I turned a Subway sandwich shop into a nonprofit organization. [*Laugh #11*] I financially fell on my face."

Surprise is the second theory of why humans laugh. A short list of humor in this category includes sheer absurdity; bad advice; exaggeration or farce; irony; puns or plays on words; screwball comedy; physical comedy; and the cousins of overstatement and understatement. People are delightfully surprised by witty incongruity or heavy shock. A few of the laughs Darren garnered through surprise humor included falling down at the beginning of his speech, addressing the contest master (emcee) from the floor, and deciding to become a comedian in response to the question "What would you dare to dream if you knew you wouldn't fail?"

The third theory is that people laugh to release strong emotions. Often, laughter is a salve to the darker emotions of embarrassment and fear. Gallows, or morbid, humor is explained well by the release theory; we laugh to dismiss fears of our own mortality. Similarly, laughing at scatological or sexual humor relieves embarrassment. While Darren was lying on the stage, he built tension by making his audience uncomfortable. After standing up, he released the tension by saying, "What do you do when you fall on your face? Do you try and jump right up and hope no one noticed?" [*Laugh #3*] In addition, he turned a word that signals pain, *ouch*, into a trigger word that drew laughter each time he said it.

These three theories—release, superiority, and surprise—explain nearly every type of humor. But when you think of these as a Venn diagram of three partially overlapping circles, it is clear that though most jokes are best explained by one theory, many jokes work on two levels and some on all three. Self-deprecating humor, the easiest type to deploy, always hits on at least two. First, it allows others to feel superior at the speaker's expense. Second, audiences expect speakers to be competent and confident. Consequently, when a speaker makes a self-deprecating remark, the audience gets a delightful surprise and responds with laughter. Often that laughter is rooted in empathy, such as when Toastmasters laugh about themselves. Certain self-deprecating humor can even include the release theory too, for example when a speaker makes light of his own illness.

## TIP 39:  Remember to riff.

With 29 laughs, Darren LaCroix racked 1 up every 16 seconds. Darren drew on the full breadth of humor types, including surprise, superiority, and release. Of Darren's 29 laughs, 8 were principally rooted in superiority (#9, #10, #11, #13, #14, #21, #23, and #28), 12 in surprise (#1, #2, #5, #6, #8, #12, #16, #17, #19, #22, #26, and #29), and 9 in release (#3, #4, #7, #15, #18, #20, #24, #25, and #27). And Darren told clusters of jokes, known to comedians as riffing. The objective is to get one laugh, pause for a moment to let the laughter settle down, then elaborate with an even more outrageous or extreme comment along the same vein. Most comedians strive to apply the rule of three, moving on after three successively funnier riffs. Though it is possible to push past three, only speakers like Darren with very well rehearsed material should attempt to do so in high-stakes presentations.

Twenty-three of Darren's jokes were delivered in clusters of two or more. Only six of the laughs Darren received were from stand-alone jokes. Impressively, his entire introduction is a riff that generated a cluster of seven laughs. Part 1 of his speech continued in the same vein with a succession of four laughs. Notably, Darren did not engineer any laughs into part 2 or 7 of his speech in order to give his audience a breather and to signal that those two sections conveyed his inspirational core message.

## TIP 40:  Amplify humor with vocal, physical, and facial expressiveness.

Humor is one of the most difficult skills to master in public speaking. Though daunting at first glance, writing funny material that engages the audience with a sense of surprise, release, or superiority is only half the battle. Many of us can voice brilliantly funny lines yet fail to get laughs. Why?

More often than not, the reason is due to a specific and easily fixed error in delivery. As if speaking in front of tens, hundreds, or thousands of people were not enough, the fear of telling a joke and not getting a laugh is downright terrifying. No one wants to bomb in front of friends, family, and coworkers. As a consequence, far too many speakers power through jokes without even pausing to let the audience laugh.

As crucial as silence is to capturing laughter, exaggerated vocal variety and physicality are the catalysts igniting it. Darren applied this technique by exaggerating his voice and mannerisms. For example, he assumed a serious pose with his hands on his hips, enthusiastically nodding as he said, "After four years of business school I went out and I went for the American dream. I bought a Subway sandwich shop. [*Laugh #8*] Oh, yeah. You're all impressed, I can tell." [*Laugh #9*]

Facial expressiveness is another catalyst used to accelerate laughter. Darren used his face to amplify laughter throughout his speech. As he shared his Subway sandwich shop experience, he pursed his lips and raised his eyebrows. It is worth noting that facial expressions alone are often enough to draw out sizable laughter.

## TIP 41:  All humor should further the message.

Avoid recycled jokes that have been passed down over time by comedians. These jokes rarely further a speaker's message, feel inauthentic, and risk falling flat if too many people have heard them before. Though recycled jokes are rather hard to find in the Toastmasters world championship, Willie Jones won in 1997 despite committing this error. His core message, directed at his fellow baby boomers, was to stop regretting things you have not done and to start living. He introduced the new, but complementary, theme of not taking yourself too seriously in his conclusion and supported it with the following:

> As a matter of fact, the way you should treat failure is like the preacher did when he gave his first sermon before the big preacher in the church one day. And the sermon was really bad. And the right reverend got up and told him, "That wasn't very good." And he humiliated the young preacher in front of the whole audience.
>
> And the preacher said, "I'll do better next week."
>
> The next week he came in, and he gave a second sermon, and he remembered being humiliated, and he said, "I'm not going to fail this week." He said, "My fellow parishioners. I can fail, you can fail, and the Monsignor can fail. I can sin, you can sin, and the Monsignor can sin. I can go to Hell, you can go to Hell, . . ." You know what. Don't take yourself so seriously.

Instead of telling jokes, the best way to get laughs *and* further your message is to use situational humor drawn from your personal experience. Two of our favorite types of situational humor include sharing our failures and repeating the candid dialogue of children responding to our behavior.

### TIP 42:  Pause and stay in character while the audience is laughing.

When you watch great comedians like Bill Cosby, Jerry Seinfeld, and Kathy Griffin, notice that they generally have two modes while they wait in silence for laughter to subside. When they are playing a character, they remain in character with limited or no movement; the exception is when movement is part of the joke. When they get a laugh for something they say while not in character, they hold a very mild smile and either stay relatively still or move to a new stage location.

●   ●   ●   ●   ●

A speaker uses humor to build rapport and relax tension, thereby increasing the likelihood that the audience will accept the core message. As you will discover in the next chapter, world champions understand that humor is one technique among many to inspire people.

## CHAPTER 5

# Amplifying Emotional Texture

**TIP 43:** **Bring your audience through the broadest possible range of emotions.**

Classifying emotion is slippery business. Two distinguished researchers, Paul Ekman and Robert Plutchik, have espoused overlapping but not identical theories. By studying facial microexpressions across cultures, Ekman identified six primary emotions: anger, disgust, fear, happiness, sadness, and surprise. Plutchik, in his visually memorable "Wheel of Emotions," posited eight paired emotions: joy-sadness, trust-disgust, fear-anger, and surprise-anticipation.

We have found that a hybrid of the two is most effective for speech development. Our seven emotions of speaking are anger, disgust, fear, happiness, love, sadness, and surprise. (We eliminated anticipation because it typically triggers other emotions; for instance, anticipation of something pleasant feels like happiness. Additionally, we transformed trust into love because love is the more powerful and common emotion elicited in public speaking.

The Wheel of Emotions treats love as a composite of joy and trust, but we have all seen love exist without either.)

Most winning Toastmasters speeches manage to hit every one of those seven emotions in as little as five to seven minutes, but that takes incredibly careful writing. Focus on only one or two of these emotions, and you risk an audience disengaging from your message. As we have indicated at the beginning of each paragraph below, Randy Harvey (2004) moved his audience from emotion to emotion to engage their hearts. He chose love as his core theme, and most of his speech triggers positive feelings. However, he peppered his speech with anger, disgust, fear, sadness, and surprise to amplify the warm moments through contrast.

## Lessons from Fat Dad (2004)

| Central message(s) | Love |
|---|---|
| Duration | 7.45 minutes |
| Words per minute | 108 |
| Laughs per minute | 2.82 |

### (INTRODUCTION)

[*Surprise*] When I was seven we drove to my cousin's for dinner and to show off Fat Dad's new car, a 1960 Ford Fairlane. I fell asleep in the backseat, and my folks left me sleeping as they went on up to the house. When I woke up, I stumbled out of the car and headed for the porch. [*Loud woofing*] I was surrounded by a pack of black and tan hunting hounds. My heart jumped. And then, so did I! First to the trunk . . . and then to the roof . . . of his new car.

[*Fear*] Mr. Contest Chair, fellow Toastmasters and guests, I was frozen like a treed raccoon. I was bawling and screaming. The hounds were circling and howling. An ugly one-eyed dog clawed and scratched its way onto the trunk. Its yellow teeth snapping and foaming. I was standing in water. It was mine.

[*Love*] His claws screeched and slipped on the glass when I heard, "Son," and I dove at the voice to be caught in Fat Dad's arms. Safety was a flannel shirt that smelled of cherry tobacco and a thunderous bellow that scattered hounds like cottonseed on the wind.

### (PART 1)

[*Love*] The next morning Fat Dad was buffing the scratches out of his new car. I said, "Fat Dad, I'm sorry you had to rescue me." He scooped me up in his big arms and said, "Son, in life sometimes you're the catcher, sometimes you're the caught." When you love somebody, their trouble is your trouble. Fat Dad was my daddy, and that loving nickname Fat Dad has been handed down through four generations to the men in my family.

### (PART 2)

[*Happiness*] When I was 16, Fat Dad bought me a 1963 Volkswagen Beetle, white tires, chrome wheels.

[*Surprise followed by disgust*] I was driving it one sunny afternoon, listening to Simon and Garfunkel on the eight track, "Cecilia, you're breaking my heart," when a humongous horsefly shot through the window into my mouth and down my throat. [*Coughing, gagging*] It came back up lodged in my right nostril. What would you do with a horsefly buzzing in your nose taking bites the size of Texas? I steered with my knees trying to fire that bug out of my nose.

[*Fear*] The car shot to the left. Then it catapulted back to the right. Chopped down Morrison's fence, sailing across their yard right at Mossburger's fountain where Mary Poppins stood

holding her umbrella, pouring water from a can. I hit that fountain so hard I launched it like Sputnik. Mary Poppins hovered
briefly, then went down faster than a spoonful of sugar.

[*Anger*] The Morrisons and the Mossburgers . . . they were a
bit excited, not Fat Dad. He rode in like the cavalry, made peace
with the neighbors. I sat on a rock in shock.

[*Love*] As Fat Dad put his arm around me, I burst into tears.
"Shhhhh, we can fix the fence. I'll buy another fountain. We can
even replace that old car. Those are just things, but I could never
replace you. Besides, the town will be talking about this for
weeks." The lesson? Love.

### (PART 3)

[*Love*] Teenage boys, they don't always think about cars.
Sometimes they think about girls. Fat Dad overheard me and
my buddies bragging about our adventures with women; not
being the shy type he joined right in, listened for a while, and
then like ice water thrown on you in a cold shower said, "Boys,
real men love for a lifetime, not for a moment." Ruined the whole
conversation.

[*Love*] But Fat Dad loved my mama. When they walked in the
garden or when they sat on the sofa, their hands always seemed
to find each other, and when Mama was sitting watching TV, Fat
Dad would come up behind her, wrap his strong arms around
her, rest his chin on her shoulder, kiss her on the cheek. As a
teenager I couldn't believe old people carried on that way, but
Fad Dad's love was more than romance.

[*Sadness*] When my mama battled the cancer that eventually took her life, Fat Dad, like a good shepherd caring for
a wounded lamb, fed and bathed, read and sang to her. And
when my mama's sunset fell and turned to starlight, Fat Dad
held her close, whispered words of love and faith to calm her
fear. Fat Dad's love for my mama was a gift to my wife and
children because watching him I learned to love them for
a lifetime.

**(CONCLUSION)**

[*Sadness*] This year I had my first Father's Day without Fat Dad, and I miss him.

[*Love*] But the lessons he taught me will last a lifetime. When you love, sometimes you're the catcher, sometimes you're the caught. When there's trouble, love rushes in, wraps its strong arms around you. Real men, well, they love for a lifetime not for a moment.

[*Love*] Fellow Toastmasters, the lesson is love, and I'm proud to tell you my children call me Fat Dad.

---

## TIP 44: Match your voice, body, and face to the emotional tone in each part of your speech.

The most fundamental principle of public speaking, which we repeatedly reference, is that you do not have to remember (or even know) any of the mechanics of public speaking if you simply become mindful of having an authentic conversation with your audience. This principle guides what to do with your voice, body, and face during each part of your speech. If you are telling a story, feel what you felt. If you are talking about research, allow your inner child to express her wonder. Passion complements professionalism.

Randy shared the following with us about finding authenticity:

*When I first met Ryan Avery, he told me his goal was to win the World Championship of Public Speaking. I looked him in the eye and said, "Well, if that's the case, then I can't help you." Participating in the contest is about identifying the message that's central to the core of who you are and then developing your ability to present that message when you speak to people. Speak from your heart, and the world will listen. Lead from your heart, and the world with follow. Follow your heart, and you'll always know happiness.*

*During the 10 weeks I worked with Ryan prior to his victory, my goal was to prepare him to give the central message that exemplified who he is and what he's about. Deliver a message that's uniquely you, not one borrowed from someone else. When you can communicate that from the core of your being, you speak with authenticity. That authenticity is unshakable, unmovable, and immutable.*

*I remember very clearly that my public speaking journey began in elementary school and our teacher played a speech from a recent demonstration in Washington, D.C. The speaker was Martin Luther King Jr. delivering his "I Have a Dream" speech. The hair on my arms stood up. What I observed there, with Martin Luther King's speech and later when I studied the speeches of John Kennedy, Winston Churchill, and Mahatma Gandhi, was that these individuals believed so strongly in their message that they would sacrifice their lives before they would give up.*

*People are not going to follow someone who's got the same message as everyone else. What people look for is an individual that has a unique message; people want to see that the individual is living their message. Where the public speaking comes in is developing the skills to communicate that message in the most effective way so that it touches the hearts and minds of people and changes the course of human history. That is not something you can achieve in a weekend seminar.*

*When I work with executives and politicians on developing communication skills, I say, "Let's start writing down all the questions that you get day in and day out." Everybody has half a dozen to a dozen questions that they get asked all the time. For me, as a lawyer, the questions are "Do I have a case?" "Will I win?" "What are the damages?"*

*Once we identify the questions they commonly receive, I work with them to find their core by asking them a series of three specific questions. Let's say I'm working with a politician and the question that he is asked is, "Do you believe in the sales tax?" Well, depending on their political persuasion, they may have different views. The first question I ask them is, "Who are you?" That question reveals what they believe in at a deep, philosophical level. If he is a conservative, he'll believe that no tax is a good tax. If he's a liberal, he might believe taxes are appropriate to support endeavors for the less fortunate. The second question I ask them is, "What are you about?" That question reveals the rules they live their life by. These are the core principles that they would sacrifice their lives to defend before they would compromise. A liberal politician might answer, "I believe that those of us who are fortunate have a responsibility to help those who are less fortunate." Finally, I ask them "Where did you learn this?" to uncover stories to support their message. You should be able to go back in time to find where you learned a particular core value. You can find a person or an event that established it.*

We understand that being authentic is easier said than done, especially when you are nervous. So that you can fake it until you make it, consider how Randy conveyed his emotions during his winning speech:

*Surprise.* When Randy said, "I was surrounded by a pack of black and tan hunting hounds. My heart jumped," his hands were protectively raised in front of him, he leaned back, his eyes were huge, and his mouth was open.

*Fear.* When Randy said, "I was frozen like a treed raccoon," his eyes were wide open, mouth agape, shoulders raised, elbows tucked in, fists clenched, knees close together, speech fast, and voice high pitched.

*Love.* When Randy said, "Son, in life sometimes you're the catcher, sometimes you're the caught," his face wore a calm, soft smile, his body was relaxed with his hands touching his heart, his voice was soft, and he spoke slowly.

*Happiness.* When Randy said, "When I was 16, Fat Dad bought me a 1963 Volkswagen Beetle, white tires, chrome wheels," his eyes widened as his smile grew, his arm and body movements were more energetic, and his rate of speaking increased.

*Disgust.* When Randy said, "a humongous horsefly shot through the window into my mouth and down my throat," he coughed and gagged, his eyes narrowed, his nose scrunched, his speech slowed, and his voice became soft and low.

*Anger.* When Randy said, "The Morrisons and the Mossburgers . . . they were a bit excited," he was still in character as a frightened teenager who had just crashed his car. When people are angry, they assume an aggressive posture, taking up more space with their arms and legs. Their eyes narrow, their nostrils flare, their teeth flash, and their speech becomes fast and loud.

*Sadness.* When Randy said, "When my mama battled the cancer that eventually took her life, Fat Dad, like a good shepherd caring for a wounded lamb, fed and bathed, read and sang to her," his eyelids and the corners of his mouth dropped, and he spoke slowly in a soft and low voice.

## TIP 45:  Express your emotions, but don't lose control.

If a speaker is not able to express emotions, then the audience will never be able to experience them either. Every speaker who makes it to the stage in the finals of the World Championship of Public Speaking is able to get emotionally worked up in front of an audience, but less-practiced speakers often struggle with too little emotional disclosure for a number of reasons.

The most common is nervousness. When we are nervous, we lose expressiveness in the face and voice. Nervousness even restrains our range of physical movement. Even when the nervousness subsides, some speakers fear that showing emotion exposes their egos. That is true. But so what? The price we pay for encasing our ego in a three-foot-thick wall of concrete is that we fail to connect with the audience, and that is too dear a price to pay in any setting.

Randy spoke of losing his mother and his father with a tenderness that helped him remain composed. A number of other world champions came close to crossing the line past which one cannot maintain emotional control—none more so than David Henderson (2010), who spoke through tears for most of his speech as he relived the tragic loss of his childhood friend.

Of the seven emotions of speaking, five actually allow you to talk more—anger, disgust, happiness, love, and surprise. In contrast, fear and sadness make you clam up. It is pretty hard to get overwhelmed by the fear that you relive when telling a story. Hence, the only emotion that typically poses a significant risk for speakers is sadness. Watching a Toastmasters contest can be a bit like watching a Shakespearean tragedy; there are countless stories of losing loved ones to incurable illness, accident, or simply old age. However, sob stories rarely win—only 4 of the past 17 champions played the tragedy card. Often, when aspiring speakers think of emotion, they narrowly focus on sadness, using their audiences' tears as evidence of success. However, there are six other emotions that captivate equally if not better.

•   •   •   •   •

Emotion is rooted in language. But language, as explored in the next chapter, plays a broader role as an aid to comprehension, sensory experience, and sticky messaging.

## CHAPTER 6

# Crafting Engaging Language

**TIP 46:** **Use simple words and short sentences to express your message.**

If you go to a Toastmasters club anywhere in the world tonight, you will likely be encouraged to use the word of the day. More often than not, it is a "$10 word" like *quixotic, sanguine,* or *mellifluous.* It is a fun game that encourages quick thinking on the part of each speaker and active listening on the part of the audience. Also, there is often a 100 percent guarantee of laughter when a speaker uses the word, since it relieves audience tension.

The problem with the word-of-the-day concept is that it perpetuates the myth that great speakers need extensive vocabularies. A speaker's job is to connect emotionally with the people in the audience and, the hope is, inspire them to look at the world differently, not to impress an audience with vocabulary (or anything else for that matter). If a speaker taxes the audience's cognitive processing ability, no connection will be made.

Devised by Rudolf Flesch and developed by J. Peter Kincaid, the Flesch-Kincaid (F-K) grade-level algorithm was first used in

1978 to measure the difficulty of technical manuals used by the U.S. military. Today, it forms the basis of the readability statistics in Microsoft Word. Measured using the F-K test, winning speeches over the preceding 17 years ranged at grade levels between 3.5 and 7.7, equivalent to the average reading level of a 9- to 13-year-old.

Contrary to what you might assume, the F-K score is not based on a dictionary. It does not know that *genre, chord structures,* and *improvisation* are more complex than *type, harmony,* and *creativity.* The grade level goes up for two simple reasons. The first is because the text contains long sentences. The second is because the text contains a large number of multisyllabic words. Listeners prefer short sentences composed of short words.

Champion David Brooks (1990) is widely acknowledged as an artist with words. His speech, "Silver Bullets," stressed the importance of returning to the core values of honor, integrity, and self-respect. David's speech contains simple words and short sentences and is written to be accessible to a fifth grader. It averages 9.7 words per sentence and has a scant 7.7 percent of words with three or more syllables. (In David's speech, we have noted, in brackets and capital letters, and underlined his use of certain rhetorical techniques that we will elaborate on in Tip 49.)

# Silver Bullets (1990)

| | |
|---|---|
| **Central message(s)** | Honor |
| **Duration** | 6.76 minutes |
| **Words per minute** | 127 |
| **Laughs per minute** | 1.48 |

**(INTRODUCTION)**

"You can't go home again." That's what Thomas Wolfe said.

But ladies and gentlemen, I was born and raised in Dallas, Texas! And I've come home. And it feels good.

Mr. Chairman, fellow Toastmasters and guests: [*CONSONANCE*] In case you're wondering, yes, some of us really do dress this way down here. . . . The tuxedo is a symbol of respect. And the jeans? [*ASSONANCE*] Well, that just means we put just a little too much of our oil money into Texas savings and loans.

[*ANAPHORA*] It's the matter of respect, however, that is the foundation of my message today. And in a time in which the famous are becoming infamous, when contemptible behavior has become commonplace, maybe it's time we looked beyond mere symbols. Maybe it's time we all came home again to a few values we seem to have left behind.

**(PART 1)**

First, let me tell you what I left behind. I said I was raised in Dallas. Truth is, I was raised just a few miles south of here in a tiny town named DeSoto . . . which, as far as I know, is the only town in the state named for a car. [*EPISTROPHE*] Remember Mayberry? Well, it was a lot like Mayberry, only not nearly as cosmopolitan.

But it was home for the first half of my life. The place where my two brothers and I learned values and principles; [*HENDIATRIS*] where we learned about honor, integrity, and self-respect.

And from whom did we learn these values? [*Pause.*] [*ANADIPLOSIS*] From television! Yes, television, because that's where our heroes lived. Oh sure, our parents tried to teach us the same lessons, but we were kids, so we paid attention to television. Remember now, this was 30 years ago and we had different role models than . . . Bart Simpson and Teenage Mutant Ninja Turtles.

[*HENDIATRIS*] No, this was the era of <u>Superman, Sky King, and Roy Rogers</u>. My brothers and I watched their shows, and when they were over, we went outside to reenact them. My older brother, of course, would be Roy Rogers. So, naturally, I got to be . . . Dale Evans. Oh, it wasn't so bad, really . . . our little brother got to be Trigger.

Yes, we had great role models [back] then. But the best role model of all was—wait—let's see if you remember. [*CONSONANCE*] I'm going to start a <u>famous phrase,</u> and I want you to <u>finish</u> it when I give you this cue. [*Hand sign as if twirling a lasso*]

[*CONSONANCE*] But remember, we do things BIG down here, so I want them to hear you from <u>Singapore</u> to "<u>San Antone</u>." Are you ready? Then return with me now to those thrilling days of yesteryear . . .

A fiery horse with the speed of light, a cloud of dust, and a hearty: [*Audience response: Hi-yo Silver, away . . .*]

Yes! The Lone Ranger rides again. Makes you feel good, doesn't it? [*ANADIPLOSIS; HENDIATRIS*] Well, from the moment I heard those words, I was swept <u>away</u> . . . <u>away</u> to a time and place where <u>honor and integrity and self-respect</u> were valued and rewarded.

[*ANAPHORA*] <u>I wanted to</u> grow up to be just like the Lone Ranger. <u>I wanted to</u> ride a fiery white stallion. <u>I wanted to</u> wear a mysterious black mask. And <u>I wanted to</u> shoot silver bullets.

[*ANADIPLOSIS*] But more than this, I wanted to be like the Lone Ranger because even as a child, I knew there was something special about <u>a person who stood</u> tall—<u>a person who stood</u> for what was right.

### (PART 2)

But then something happened, and everything changed: I grew up. [*CONSONANCE; ANAPHORA*] And as <u>I learned</u> to separate <u>fantasy from fact, I learned</u> a <u>terrifying truth. I learned</u> that the heroes of a modern world were but mere mortals, and oh what fools these mortals be.

Why, in just the past three years we've seen an Olympic athlete stripped of his gold medals because he used drugs. We've seen not one, but two television ministers fall from grace. [*CONSONANCE*] We've seen <u>billionaires bankrupted</u> by greed.

And we've seen Donald Trump . . . be Donald Trump.

[*HENDIATRIS*] <u>Honor, integrity, self-respect?</u> It seemed we'd left them all behind.

### (PART 3)

Until last year. And, once again, I saw it on television.

June 3, 1989. Beijing. After days of peaceful protest, a column of armored tanks rumbled into Tiananmen Square. [*ANAPHORA*] <u>Everyone</u> in their path ran for safety. <u>Everyone</u> . . . but one.

About a hundred yards down the street, standing firmly on the center line, one man remained. He stood alone.

The tanks kept coming . . . their massive steel tracks clawing at the center line. The man stood firm. The tanks came closer . . . and closer . . . until the lead tank closed to within inches. And the man stood tall.

And then . . . the tanks . . . stopped.

I wanted to cheer . . . but I was choked by tears. Who was this man who moved me so? [*EPISTROPHE*] I wanted <u>to know</u>. Ah, but then I remembered . . . you're not supposed <u>to know</u> . . . the Lone Ranger's name.

### (CONCLUSION)

Oh, in that one triumphant moment, he took us back to yesteryear—to a wonderful time and place where people stood for what they believed in—no matter what the cost.

[*HENDIATRIS*] And he reminded us of what we've all known since we were children: to make a difference, all we need are three silver bullets: <u>honor, integrity, and self-respect.</u>

[*CONSONANCE*] Yes . . . in more <u>ways</u> than <u>one</u>, we <u>can come</u> home again.

### TIP 47:   Intensify your language with vivid images and sensory detail.

Using simple words does not mean that you need to compromise on the emotional intensity of your language. In his outstanding book *The Presentation Secrets of Steve Jobs*, Carmine Gallo describes the technology pioneer's language as simple, concrete, and emotional. The key to building emotional intensity is the use of descriptive adjectives and adverbs. Think of Steve Jobs using the words *amazing, incredible,* and *unbelievable.*

Our job as speakers is to captivate our audience from start to finish by delivering a meaningful message. We want to capture our listeners' imagination and involve them in our story by making them feel truly connected. To really engage your audience, ask yourself, "Can I smell, taste, or feel my speech?" Use all five senses. David incorporated sensory language throughout his speech, and one could actually hear, see, and feel the tanks rumbling into Tiananmen Square.

### TIP 48:   Encapsulate your core message in a memorable catchphrase and repeat often.

Though there may be rare times when speakers should let their core message subtly sink in, the Toastmasters International Speech Contest is not one of them. The question is not whether to have a catchphrase; the question is how to construct and deliver it.

Between 1995 and 2011, 12 of the 17 winners had clearly distinguishable catchphrases. Of those 12 speakers, 8 used their speech title as their catchphrase, resulting in three huge benefits. First, using a catchphrase as your title forces you to stay on message. It makes the spine of your speech unambiguously clear so you can edit thoughtfully. Second, and more important, following this approach makes your core message crystal clear to your audience. Third, in a competitive speaking environment, the judges need only look to your title to recall the power of your speech.

The most effective catchphrases are short, repeated, rhythmic, and actionable. David's catchphrase, "honor, integrity, and self-respect," met only the first two criteria; nonetheless it successfully cemented his "silver bullet" values into the minds of his audience. Many other catchphrases from world championship speeches, including (coauthor of this book) Ryan's catchphrase, "trust is a must," met all four criteria.

## TIP 49:  Polish your speech with rhetorical wordplay.

There is a vast array of rhetorical devices that you can use to enhance your speech. Though some have unfamiliar names, you will recognize many in the list below as the most common types found in modern public speaking:

- *Assonance and consonance.* These kissing cousins refer to the repetition of the same sound two or more times in rapid succession. Assonance is the repetition of vowel sounds; consonance is the repetition of consonant sounds. We can see an example of consonance in David's speech when he repeats the *f* sound three times in the line, "I'm going to start a <u>famous phrase</u>, and I want you to <u>finish</u>."

- *Anaphora.* This is the repetition of the same word or words at the beginning of successive phrases or sentences. An example is David's "<u>maybe it's time</u> we looked beyond mere symbols. <u>Maybe it's time</u> we all came home again to a few values we seem to have left behind."

- *Epistrophe.* This is the same concept as anaphora applied to the ends of phrases or sentences. An example is David's "I wanted <u>to know</u>. Ah, but then I remembered . . . you're not supposed <u>to know</u> . . . the Lone Ranger's name."

- *Symploce.* This combines the anaphora and epistrophe. While David Brooks did not use this device, champion Jock

Elliott (2011) did with, "<u>Sometimes</u> in the springtime of life when young blood courses through vibrant <u>veins,</u> <u>sometimes</u> later in life when more sluggish blood cruises through varicose <u>veins</u>."

- *Anadiplosis.* This is the repetition of the last word of one sentence at or near the beginning of the next. An example is David's "I knew there was something special about <u>a person who stood</u> tall—<u>a person who stood</u> for what was right."

- *Hendiatris.* This is the use of three words in succession to express a single concept. David's catchphrase, "honor, integrity, and self-respect," is an example expressing core values, as is "Superman, Sky King, and Roy Rogers," expressing nostalgic television heroes.

In addition to these fancier rhetorical techniques, good old repetition of phrases or sentences is a powerful way to underscore key messages.

### TIP 50: Use single items for attention, pairs for contrast, lists of three for harmony, and long lists to build intensity.

Single items command attention, pairs emphasize contrast, and threes accentuate similarity. There are also times when very long lists are appropriate. Consider the following portion of Craig Valentine's (1999) winning speech:

> But you've turned your back on it [your spirit], and you wonder why you have your ups and downs and goods and bads and backs and forths and bottoms and tops and ins and outs . . . and the bottom line is you've turned your back on your spirit and that's why you stumble and why you fall.

Craig's verbally acrobatic list, delivered very rapidly, builds intensity to a boiling point. Then, following a dramatic pause and a slow rehashing of what he said, he provides the cure:

*Silence, that's it. Silence, you're trying to tell me that I never take the time to just be silent and still and listen to my spirit.*

## TIP 51:  Avoid quoting famous people.

One of the persistent myths among Toastmasters around the world is that talented speakers must be able to sling famous quotations at the drop of a hat. However, that belief is sorely misguided. In almost all circumstances, using famous quotes is unoriginal and clichéd. Rattling off quotes is most damaging because the practice is inauthentic. Audiences want to hear *you*, to listen to your stories. If they want quotes, then they can pick up a copy of *Bartlett's Familiar Quotations.*

Besides David Brooks's skillful citation of Thomas Wolfe more than 20 years ago, there are precious few examples of champions slinging canned quotations. Mark Brown (1995) opened with, "You never get a second chance to make a first impression," a familiar quote of unknown attribution, and Mark Hunter (2009) referenced Deepak Chopra, also in the body of his speech.

A rare exception to the "no-quotations" rule is in the introduction of Jock Elliott's (2011) winning speech, which starts: "John Lau says in his Facebook page that 'Everyone has a best friend at each stage of their life. Only a lucky few have the same one.'" This quote works for two reasons. The first is novelty; it is unlikely that anyone in the audience had ever heard it before. The second is that it customized his speech, one that he had polished many, many times over the course of several years, for that particular audience on that specific day. Who is John Lau? He is a past international president of Toastmasters International *and* was the emcee of the contest on the day Jock won!

## TIP 52:  Surprise your audience with misdirection.

A second exception to the no-quotations rule is found in Jim Key's (2003) speech, which contains the overarching message that it is never too late to follow your dreams.

One of the great principles of public speaking is that your listeners should not be able to finish your sentence unless you actively want them to. Misdirection takes this one clever step further. After Jim had used the word *dream* the ninth of twenty-four times, he proceeded: "Ladies and gentlemen, we were meant to dream. We were meant to dream. Dr. Martin Luther King Jr., one of the greatest dreamers of our age, said . . ." At this point, everybody in the audience was expecting Jim to say, "I have a dream!" Instead, he surprised the audience by using another quotation:

> *"The time is always right to do what is right," and that means that if it was right for us to dream as children, then it's just as right for us to dream as adults.*

Like Jock's quote, Jim's quote shares a sense of novelty because few, if any, in the audience were familiar with it. It comes from a lesser known speech that Dr. King delivered at Oberlin College in October 1964. Of course, the other reason this quote works is because of misdirection.

## TIP 53:  Ruthlessly remove all language that does not further your message.

David Brooks admires speeches where "there's not a word or thought misplaced." His admiration is well founded because speakers quite naturally fall in love with their own words, phrases, ideas, examples, . . . well almost everything they write or say. But great writers recognize that you have to ruthlessly remove all language that does not further a message. Sir Arthur Quiller-Couch said it best: "Whenever you feel an impulse to perpetrate a piece of exceptionally fine writing, obey it—wholeheartedly—and delete it before sending your manuscript to press. Murder your darlings."[1]

Seeing your writing in an objective light is easier said than done, so we offer two approaches for murdering your darlings. The first is to find an editor with the good judgment to see when you have drifted off message and with the strength to convince you to hit *Delete*. The second is to follow Jock Elliott's advice to "walk away from your preparation and then come back to the speech cold and say: 'Yes, lovely as it is, I will keep this idea for the future because it is good, but it does not live in this speech.'" Keeping the macabre metaphor going, writers express this concept as "Write in white heat, but revise in cold blood."

## TIP 54:  Build in time for audience reactions.

When Sean Shannon delivered Hamlet's 260-word soliloquy "To be or not to be" in 23.8 seconds in August 1995, he became the world's fastest talker at 655 words per minute. Though an amazing curiosity, his performance lacked the emotional intensity of Sir Laurence Olivier's 1948 cinematic masterpiece. Mr. Olivier delivered the same passage in 3 minutes and 18 seconds, or 79 words per minute.

In the Toastmasters world championship, speakers must deliver their speech within 5 to 7 minutes, with a 30-second buffer on either side. Contestants see a green light at 5 minutes followed by a yellow light at 6 minutes. The red light comes on at 7 minutes and stays on; there is no indication provided if the disqualifying threshold of 7 minutes and 30 seconds is breached.

Many speakers have had victory stolen from their grasp in prior years mainly because of failing to adequately account for audience reaction time, particularly for the delay added by laughter. At each level of the contest, as the audience size increases, speakers have no alternative than to trim words.

Over the past 17 years, the average champion delivered 892 words in 7 minutes and 15 seconds. That works out to just under 125 words per minute. At 127 words per minute, David Brooks (1990) was right at the average.

The fastest champion in recent history was Craig Valentine (1999), at 198 words per minute. His call to action was that everybody should take five minutes of contemplative silence each day. To build tension for the extended moments of silence in his speech, he delivered artful bursts of words. However, he knew that his audience would not fully comprehend what he was saying. So, after each burst, he slowed down and repeated his message.

Vikas Jhingran (2007) and Brett Rutledge (1998) were at the low end, speaking at a rate of 98 and 99 words per minute, respectively.

## TIP 55: Craft a memorable title that triggers insatiable curiosity.

A speaker's ability to engage the audience begins before a step is taken onto the stage. Strive to trigger audience curiosity with a "Why?" or "How?" prompt in your speech title. Titles that prompt the question "Who?" or "What?" or "Where?" are generally less potent.

The most powerful open-ended question to incite in a motivational speech is "Why?" Even when people have paid to hear you speak, they hold an invisible shield up until you give them a reason to drop it. Prompting your listeners to ask *why* invites them to lower that shield. The second most powerful open-ended question is "How?" If your talk is about happiness, then instilling a burning desire in audience members to understand *how* signals that you will deliver your magic recipe for blissful living.

To know what constitutes a great title, you merely need to peruse the past 26 years of winning speeches. In descending order of impact, here are the types of titles that have been used: maxims, imperatives, verb phrases, adjective phrases, exclamations, noun phrases, and sentences.

Maxims are powerful because they simultaneously deliver the core message of the speech while prompting not only how and why but also other questions. Examples of maxims include Jim Key's "Never Too Late" (2003), Otis Williams Jr.'s "It's Possible" (1993), Don Johnson's "A Many-Splendored Thing" (1989), and Harold Patterson's "The Pain Passes" (1987).

Imperatives are typically as potent as maxims: LaShunda Rundles's "Speak!" (2008), David Nottage's "Get Up" (1996), and Dana LaMon's "Take a Chance" (1992). Jerry Starke's "Please Don't Walk on Mother's Roses" (1988) is far more subtle and therefore far more memorable.

A close third in terms of impact is verb phrases. Edward Hearn's "Bouncing Back" (2006) prompts why, how, and who. The same holds true for Morgan McArthur's "Stuck to a Bucket" (1994). McArthur's title has the same subtle yet memorable quality that Jerry Starke's title had.

Adjective phrases and exclamations are rare. In fact, there has only been one of each in the past 26 years. Jock Elliott's adjective title "Just So Lucky" (2011) described a positive state of being. Darren LaCroix's exclamation "Ouch!" (2001) did the opposite for pain. Each title was inextricably linked to the content of the speech. Jock Elliott shared how lucky he was to have the friends of his blood, the friends of his times, and the friends of his heart. Darren LaCroix used the physical pain of falling down as a metaphor for having the resilience to persevere in the face of failure, doubt, and rejection.

Though not the most stimulating or powerful, nouns and noun phrases are the most common titles used in winning Toastmasters speeches. Nonetheless, noun-based titles typically prompt the question "What?" Intangible nouns make for more thought-provoking titles than tangible nouns. This is highlighted in the following group of winning titles based on intangible concepts: Vikas Jhingran's "The Swami's Question" (2007), Lance Miller's "The Ultimate Question" (2005), Randy Harvey's "Lessons from Fat Dad" (2004), Dwayne Smith's "Music in the Key of Life" (2002), Craig Valentine's "The Key to Fulfillment" (1999), and Mark Brown's "A Second Chance" (1995).

Next, consider the group of tangible noun titles that spotlight people, places, and things. David Henderson's "The Aviators" (2010) focused on people. Brett Rutledge suggested a location with "My Little World" (1998). Rounding out the list of tangibles are thing-based titles, including Mark Hunter's "A Sink Full of Green Tomatoes" (2009), Ed Tate's "One of Those Days" (2000), Willie Jones's "A Warm Boot" (1997), and David Brooks's "Silver Bullets" (1990).

Full sentences put the speaker at an immediate disadvantage because they are by definition closed ended. That is not to say that you will not win; it is just going to be that much more challenging. Two speeches in this category that have won are David Ross's "The Train's Still Rollin'" (1991) and Arabella Bengson's "We Can Be Pygmalion" (1986).

The trait common to these winning titles is that they prime you beforehand by inciting curiosity and then persist afterward by being sensory. In addition, a memorable title needs to stand out from all the other speeches in the contest. Since most speakers choose nouns, choose something more unusual and zig when they zag.

Ryan originally entitled his speech "Promise Me," but after intense practice and rewrites, he found that title was not strong enough. Make sure you choose a title that imparts something valuable. "Promise Me" has little meaning to an audience. Moreover, the title does not even suggest what the speech is about. "Trust Is a Must" is effective because it voices a core value that everyone holds dear. It is memorable because it grabs attention.

The preceding advice applies to titling motivational speeches in a captive environment. But how should you title a speech in a way that entices people to *choose* to hear your speech, as would happen if you were speaking at a conference where your talk is one of multiple being delivered in simultaneous tracks?

Like it or not, people judge a speech by its title. When you are competing for eyeballs, craft a speech title that is short, specific, urgent, and audience centric. Conference organizers typically do not disclose attendance at individual track sessions, so we turn to the world of Internet marketing to support our advice. Consider the top

10 blog posts of 2012 published by HubSpot Inc., a web marketing software vendor that published over 900 articles during that year, receiving more than 8.7 million visitors[2]:

- The 10 Greatest Marketing Campaigns of All Time

- 11 Simple (But Critical) Tips for Creating Better Landing Pages

- 8 Dangerous (But Common) Misconceptions About Email Marketing

- 13 Hilarious Examples of Truly Awful Stock Photography

- The History of Marketing: An Exhaustive Timeline

- 17 Examples of Twitter Brand Page Backgrounds to Inspire You

- 10 Companies That Totally Nailed Their Taglines

- Why You Need Marketing Analytics, Not Web Analytics

- 15 Things People Absolutely Hate About Your Website

- The Ultimate Cheat Sheet for Mastering LinkedIn

Just glancing through the list, you probably noticed a few patterns. The titles are all short, averaging only 8 words and 53 characters. Most of the titles (70 percent) include a number. Though most of the numbers in these blog post titles are large, ranging from 8 to 17, we advise that speeches should not exceed 3 to 5 items, or you risk both going long and overwhelming your audience. Taking a page from what Apple founder Steve Jobs was famous for, the titles use positive and negative superlatives to trigger insatiable curiosity, including *greatest, ultimate, hilarious, exhaustive, totally nailed, dangerous,* and *absolutely hate.* The titles also variously convey a sense of urgency (*critical, need*), ease (*simple*), and entertainment (*hilarious*). Finally, the titles unambiguously highlight reader-centric value in the form of how-to tips, cautionary examples to avoid, and highly effective examples to learn from.

## TIP 56: Keep your title as short as possible.

Being concise stands out as the one quality above all others that makes a speech title memorable. In 26 years, the titles of all the winning speeches averaged just three words. Two of them—"Speak!" and "Ouch!"—got the job done using only one. Six words was the longest title to win.

Do not be tempted to stand out with a very long speech title. Though not a winner, one of the most viewed Toastmasters speeches on YouTube is Andy Dooley's excellent 2006 speech, "A Short but Unbelievably Intriguing Tale of How Destiny Unexpectedly Showed Her True Colors Against the Backdrop of Pure White Snow on a Colorado Mountaintop While All Other Conditions Remained Normal." At 31 words, this title breaks the bank! Just after the contest master said "Pure White Snow," the audience erupted into rolling laughter. This approach is certainly fine for a one-off speech in any environment, and it can even help you win in the International Speech Contest up through and including the district level for its shock value rather than for its message. But judges at the highest levels are critical of attention-grabbing tricks. Note that Mr. Dooley retitled it "My Date with Destiny" when he uploaded his video for the world to see.

Titles are, of course, just one element of a speech. A bad presentation with a great title is still a bad presentation. And a great presentation with a terrible title can still be effective. But keep the odds stacked in your favor by always crafting a speech with a great title.

•    •    •    •    •

Thus far, we have focused on *what* words to say. In the next chapter, we turn to *how* to say those words.

CHAPTER 7

# Mastering Verbal Delivery

**TIP 57:** **Amplify your natural, authentic voice.**

Standing in front of tens, hundreds, or especially thousands of people, causes presenters to speak in a way that disconnects them from the emotional content of the actual words coming out of their mouths. Sometimes they can even sound somewhat muted and robotic. The best way to avoid these pitfalls is to amplify your natural delivery until you restore a natural manner of speaking.

Speaking loudly can be distracting in a small room. Conversely, presenters with softer voices are drowned out in a larger room. Although there is no perfect combination of vocal variety, projection, and pitch to suit every speaking situation, getting it right depends on synchronizing your authentic voice tuned to the venue you are speaking in with the tone of your content.

When adjusting delivery to the venue and tone of your message, it is important to express your true self while adapting your voice to help your audience better connect with your message. Sounding authentic can take some effort, but remember that it simply requires that you speak as you would to someone you care about.

If you attend the Toastmasters World Championship of Public Speaking, you might find the deep, Jamaican-accented voice of the invisible announcer to be somewhat familiar. That is because it belongs to champion Mark Brown (1995), whose baseline voice would be the envy of any radio personality. Mark's winning speech, as follows, served as a rallying cry for tolerance. (Vocal variety is identified in brackets.)

# A Second Chance (1995)

| Central message(s) | Tolerance |
|---|---|
| Duration | 6.73 minutes |
| Words per minute | 120 |
| Laughs per minute | 1.04 |

### (INTRODUCTION)

[*Baseline*] You never get a second chance to make a first impression. Mr. Toastmaster and friends, that phrase is fairly common. At first look, we automatically draw quick conclusions about people for various reasons. It could be their appearance, other people's opinions, our own preconceived ideas, or just plain ignorance. We don't always give a second chance. Let me explain.

### (PART 1)

Recently my wife, Andrea, three children, and I sat down to watch a very important film, [*high*] Beauty and the Beast. Oh, you've seen it? [*Baseline*] Then you know that this is a film that you can't watch just once. Your children won't let you. I've seen it 13 times since last Monday. Don't get me wrong. The movie is great for children. [*Slow, soft*] The music, the magic, the mystery. [*Baseline*] But the message, the message is important for all of us.

[*Slow, loud*] Picture this. The villain is the influential Gaston. He's tall, dark, handsome; I can relate to that. [*Baseline*] Gaston is in love with the beautiful Belle, but she spurns him and befriends the Beast. In a fit of jealousy, Gaston uses his influence and turns the entire village against Belle and the Beast.

Except for seeing his face once in a magic mirror, the villagers know nothing about the Beast. [*Fast, soft*] But Gaston, he fuels their fear of the unknown and whips them into a frenzy. [*Fast, loud*] This angry mob cuts down trees, and they make clubs. They brandish knives, pitchforks, and torches, and they march through the forest singing, [*melodic*] "We don't like what we don't understand. In fact it scares us, and this monster is mysterious at least. Bring your guns; bring your knives. Save your children and your wives. We'll save our village and our lives. We'll kill the Beast."

Why?

[*Baseline*] For years the Beast had lived in isolation, but no one took the time to say, [*fast, loud*] "Wait, what's he really like? Who is this beast?" [*Slow, loud*] Oh no, he wasn't given a second chance. [*Fast, loud*] And the irony is the real beast was in the hearts of the angry mob. He was a victim of the real beast—intolerance, indifference, and ignorance. [*Slow, soft*] Oh well, it's a movie, it's a fantasy, but intolerance, indifference, and ignorance are a reality. We've got to deal with it every single day. I'll give you an example.

### (PART 2)

[*Baseline*] Pat Harper, a beautiful network news anchor, reported on the plight of the homeless in New York City a few years ago. To appreciate their circumstance, she dressed as they dressed. [*Slow, soft*] She walked as they walked. She lived as they lived for several days. [*Baseline*] She carried a concealed microphone, and a hidden camera crew followed her every move.

It was Christmastime. A season of love, cheer, and goodwill. But here's what the camera saw; I'll never forget this: [*fast, soft*] it was snowing, bitterly cold, and there she sat huddled in a doorway shivering, trying to fend off the bone-chilling winds, [*baseline*] but hardly anyone noticed her. Those who did, hurried by. Some looked right at her and yet right past her. Others looked right through her as they thought, "Homeless, useless, worthless." [*Fast, soft*] No one took a second look. To them this beauty had a beastly appearance, but the real beast was in the hearts of those who treated her with disdain. [*Baseline*] Oh, yes, the beast of intolerance, indifference, and ignorance.

The sad truth is it happens all the time. I'm not just pointing fingers here because I admit I've done it too, but we don't always think about it until we come face to face with it. Perhaps you have been a victim of the beast. Think back. [*Slow, soft*] Do you remember the pain you felt when you faced intolerance just because you were different? Do you remember when you faced indifference because like Pat Harper and so many others . . . [*Fast, loud*] *Well,* your situation, that's your problem. [*Baseline*] And do you remember when you faced ignorance like that of those villagers because someone felt as they did? "We don't like what we don't understand. In fact it scares us." [*Slow, loud*] Do you remember how deeply it hurt?

### (CONCLUSION)

[*Slow, soft*] Perhaps you have participated in acts of intolerance, indifference, and ignorance. [*Baseline*] Are you guilty of feeding the beast? [*Fast, loud*] Is there someone out there, someone in your workplace, someone in your neighborhood, someone in your home who has heard your beast roar? [*Slow, soft*] My friends, do they not deserve a second chance?

[*Baseline*] As the film *Beauty and the Beast* concludes, the Beast dies. And in his place, because of Belle's love, you guessed it, a handsome prince lives. [*Fast, loud*] You see, Belle gave him a second chance. Don't you just love it? [*Baseline*] My children did. It's a perfect fairytale ending. But that story is a fantasy. Reality, as we know, is not so romantic. [*Fast, loud*] And the fantasy will never become reality unless we attack the beast, the real beast, intolerance, indifference, and ignorance. Yes, let's kill the beast! [*Slow, loud*] Because everyone deserves a second chance.

---

## TIP 58:  Add vocal variety by varying your speed and volume.

Throughout his speech, Mark matched his voice to the emotional tone of his content, resulting in natural variations in speed and volume. Because human beings are conditioned to detect change, these shifts in verbal delivery hold interest and draw attention to key points. Champion speakers most frequently change speed and volume, since those two dimensions are the easiest to alter and each combination carries a specific connotation. Let's consider Mark's variation in speed (slow to fast) and volume (soft to loud) relative to his baseline speaking voice.

Mark spoke slow and soft when he wanted to soothe his audience with feelings of warmth, wonder, and familiarity. His most memorable application of this technique occurred when he introduced Pat Harper's experiential reporting on homelessness. Speaking slower and softer with each successive sentence, Mark built deep emotional ties between his audience and Pat: "To appreciate their circumstance, she dressed as they dressed. [*Slow, soft*] She walked as they walked. She lived as they lived for several days." Note that many speakers use the slow-and-soft combination to highlight transitions, as Mark did at the end of Part 1 and at the beginning of his conclusion.

Mark spoke slow and loud when he wanted to command authority. His most dramatic application of this technique occurred in his final sentence, "Because everyone deserves a second chance." While you can speak slow and loud anytime you want to grab attention, it serves as a powerful exclamation point at the end of a speech to tell an audience that you are done, emphasize the message that matters, and issue a call to action.

Mark spoke fast and loud when he wanted to express his passion and create a sense of urgency. He shifted into this combination multiple times in railing against discrimination: "And the irony is the real beast was in the hearts of the angry mob. He was a victim of the real beast—intolerance, indifference, and ignorance."

Mark spoke fast and soft when he wanted to create suspense. Read this quote with your mental voice turned to fast and slow to feel what Pat Harper felt as a homeless person at Christmastime: "it was snowing, bitterly cold, and there she sat huddled in a doorway shivering, trying to fend off the bone-chilling winds."

### TIP 59: Vary pitch, rhythm, quality, and enunciation to create more subtle effects.

After speed and volume, pitch (from low to high) is the next most frequently tuned aspect of vocal variety. Shifting to a lower pitch is associated with seriousness, while shifting to a higher pitch conveys curiosity or surprise. Though Mark's baritone voice prevented him from reaching the higher registers, he increased his pitch with humorous impact when he said, "[*Baseline*] Recently my wife, Andrea, three children, and I sat down to watch a very important film, [*high*] *Beauty and the Beast.*

More subtle dimensions of vocal variety include rhythm, also referred to as cadence or melody, ranging from monotone to dramatic; quality, ranging from breathy to full; and enunciation, ranging from gentle to crisp. In any case, take full, deep breaths and project so that people in the last row can hear you.

### TIP 60: Eliminate filler words with practice.

Eliminating filler words is a process much like fixing a leaking pipe. You eliminate one, and soon another pops up someplace else. But a lasting fix is to pause for one beat at commas and two beats at periods and thereby eliminate the most common filler words, including *um, ah, like,* and *you know.*

To see if you use filler words at the beginning of sentences, detect the problem by watching a video of one of your speeches. If you have this problem, find a friend willing to watch you give a few speeches and have her make a noise every time you use an extraneous *so, and,* or *but.* For example, she can tap a pen on the table or snap her fingers. It should only take two or three separate sessions until you are cured.

Next, practice pausing. People use filler words to soothe anxiety by speaking constantly. You do not have to fill every moment; besides, using pauses is more professional than using filler words. Pauses allow you to think about what you will say next as well as allow your audience to digest your message.

Finally, start speaking more slowly. Practice reading aloud as slowly as you can. This will help you get used to speaking at a slower pace and allow you to notice where you typically add filler words.

### TIP 61: Use the silence of a dramatic pause to emphasize a point.

Great speakers, entrepreneurial leaders, entertainers, and even politicians know that silence is the single most effective vocal technique. American comedian Jack Benny said, "It's not so much knowing when to speak, [it's knowing] when to pause." Lance Morrow, an essayist for *Time* magazine, said, "Never forget the power of silence, that massively disconcerting pause which goes on and on and may at last induce an opponent to babble and backtrack nervously." Even race car driver Sebastian Vettel recognized the importance of a pause when he said, "Sometimes you need to press pause to let everything sink in." If you want your message to sink in with your audience, perfect the pause.

Pauses serve critical purposes because humans are hardwired to increase their attention during silence, and seasoned presenters take every advantage of their audience's evolutionary defense mechanism. The dramatic pause is most often used at the opening of a speech, but it can be used before, during, and, more often, after a significant point. Pauses allow an audience time to process what the speaker is saying. Professional speakers typically pause for one beat, the time it takes to vocalize one short musical note, at commas and for two beats at periods. To get comfortable with pausing, practice staying silent for a full three seconds between sentences. Though it will feel awkward, this exercise will make standard one- or two-second pauses feel natural to you and powerful to your audience.

### TIP 62: Nonnative speakers should embrace their accent and strive for clarity.

Public speaking is especially daunting when speaking in a language that is not your own. However, Presiyan Vasilev (2013) proved that a strong accent need not stand in the way of delivering a championship speech, provided you make a few simple adjustments.

The best way to achieve clarity as a nonnative speaker is also the easiest: slow down. Presiyan delivered his speech at 110 words per minute, which was 15 percent slower than the average native English–speaking past world champions. Another nonnative English–speaking champion, Vikas Jhingran (2007) spoke even more slowly, a measured 98 words per minute. To slow your verbal pace, elongate each word through crisp enunciation and include slight pauses between words as well as longer-than-average pauses at the ends of sentences.

Nonnative speakers do need to be mindful of word choice and nonverbal conventions. In particular, it pays to learn a few common idioms in the language you expect to present regularly in, so that the audience subconsciously embraces you. Practice with an articulate native speaker who can revise your grammatically correct but idiomatically incorrect expressions. In addition, strive to understand the most common body language differences from what you grew up with. For instance, in America, a side-to-side head wobble means "maybe," whereas in southern India it means "yes" or "I understand." If you want to go deeper into cultural etiquette, check out the definitive reference on this topic, *When Cultures Collide: Leading Across Cultures* by Richard D. Lewis.

Above all, embrace your accent as an asset rather than a liability. You might even add interest by saying and then translating a short phrase in your native language. An accent helps you stand out from the crowd and forces your listeners to pay closer attention to what you have to say than they normally would to native speakers.

.   .   .   .   .

Your ability to deliver meaningful impact depends as much on what you say as how you say it. Vocal variety and pauses naturally tie to the emotional tone of your words when you speak in your true, authentic voice. Your voice is only the first part of *how you say it.* In the next chapter, we turn to the second part—nonverbal delivery.

## CHAPTER 8

# Managing Nonverbal Delivery

### TIP 63: Power-pose just before you speak.

Social scientist and Harvard Business School professor Amy Cuddy offers advice on what you need to do *before* you enter the stage to influence how you perceive yourself and how others perceive you. She and her fellow researchers discovered two simple one-minute power poses that cause "advantaged and adaptive psychological, physiological, and behavioral changes" that allow a person to "embody power and instantly become more powerful." The researchers addressed the impact of their findings on public speaking, adding, "By simply changing physical posture, an individual prepares his or her mental and physiological systems to endure difficult and stressful situations, and perhaps to actually improve confidence and performance in situations such as interviewing for jobs, *speaking in public*, disagreeing with a boss, or taking potentially profitable risks."[1]

The two poses the researchers tested amplified expansiveness (taking up more space) and openness (keeping limbs open). Though we suspect any positions that address these two factors will have similarly positive effects, the two positions in the study are as follows: In the first power pose, each participant leaned back in her chair, clasped her hands behind her head, and put her feet up on a table. In the second power pose, each participant stood, leaning forward with her fingertips on a table and one leg in front of the other.

## TIP 64: Enter the stage with confident energy that matches your purpose.

Though Ryan Avery (this book's coauthor) was nervous when he took the stage for the final round of the 2012 World Championship of Public Speaking, you would not have known it. He trotted out with his head up and flashed a genuine smile. There is no shame in being nervous, especially with nearly 1,500 excited audience members expecting to hear one of the best speeches ever delivered. Public speaking induces anxiety no matter who you are (and anybody who tells you otherwise is flat-out lying). However, winning at the highest level of competition in Toastmasters or at work requires channeling your nervous energy into calm confidence. A speaker is judged, consciously or subconsciously, from the second he walks onto the stage to the second he walks off. Every moment counts.

History shows that it is not impossible to recover from an unfavorable first impression. Ed Hearn (2006) walked in with his head slightly down and neglected to shake the hand of the contest master. Lance Miller (2005) combined looking down several times with a nervous swaying of his hands and body.

The energy level of an entrance should reinforce the purpose of your speech. People who went on to win held their head up, sported a confident smile, and walked at a smooth pace. The same advice holds when making presentations at work, where you will generally be informing or persuading.

The energy of your entrance should also match the audience's exuberance and bridge it to the tone of your content. The 2009 world champion, Mark Hunter, holds the title for highest-energy entrance.

Because of a skiing accident 30 years prior, Mark Hunter now uses a wheelchair. He wheeled out wearing a smile of sheer delight. His eyebrows were raised high, his mouth was wide open, and his tongue even made an appearance. He set the tone appropriately for a speech sprinkled with whimsical language and physicality that tied to his core message that love is what matters.

### TIP 65:  Settle yourself and connect with your audience just before you speak.

After Ryan shook the contest master's hand, he walked to center stage and settled himself in a relaxed posture with his feet shoulder-width apart and his arms relaxed and down at his sides. When the applause dissipated, he took three seconds of silence to make eye contact with a section in the audience to his left. Turning his attention back to the center of the audience, he took a deep, but not overtly noticeable, breath and started speaking.

The techniques Ryan used to get settled and connect with his audience just before he spoke are wise practices in any public speaking situation. While fussing with papers, a projector, or a computer just before you speak is often unavoidable, you will create a favorable first impression of being in control of your material by taking the time to compose yourself, make eye contact, and fill your lungs.

### TIP 66:  Decide on a base position for your hands when *not* gesturing.

Plan what to do with your hands when you are *not* gesturing. Ryan allowed his arms and hands to relax down at his sides just before he began speaking. Over the course of his speech, he frequently returned to this base position. Ryan's "hands-down" base position is the approach of choice for speakers, in formal and informal settings, wishing to be conversational and friendly.

When you want to appear more authoritative, opt for the "stee-ple" base position, with your shoulders relaxed and your hands together at navel level. Many speakers find the steeple position to be the most natural and comfortable. Since stress often migrates to the hands, strive to keep your hands as symmetrical as possible by letting your fingers touch lightly rather than interlacing them. Similarly, to prevent white knuckles, avoid the closed-cup base position where your thumbs are locked and the remaining four fingers of each hand rest on the sides of the opposing hand. We also do not recommend pressing your palms together (the prayer base position) since that approach often comes off as arrogant.

The most important consideration is that you use whatever base position is most comfortable for you every time you speak, even if it is one that we do not recommend. Nonetheless, strive to develop two go-to base positions, one for conversational speeches and one for authoritative speeches.

## TIP 67: Hold eye contact with individual audience members for three to five seconds.

Your eyes are the window to your soul—and therefore the most important element of your body language needed to effectively deliver a presentation. If you break eye contact after only a fleeting glance, the person to whom you are speaking may lose trust in you. Conversely, if you hold eye contact for too long, the other person will feel uncomfortable. Successful speakers hold eye contact in bursts of three to five seconds with selected audience members. Since it is difficult to count and speak at the same time, figure a sentence or two as the time frame. When speaking to a very large audience, you can maintain eye contact with an entire section instead of an individual, and the time increases to a full paragraph.

Experienced speakers, like Ryan, sequentially engage individuals seated in entirely different areas of the room (not the next duck in the row). They continue this practice in a random pattern, striving to make eye contact with each person in the room at least once. With a larger audience, the people in the section surrounding the person you make eye contact with will feel as if you were looking at them as well.

## TIP 68:  Match your movement to your message and venue.

While excessive rocking or pacing is always distracting, no single rule of thumb governs the amount of movement per minute that applies to every speech. Some speeches, like Martin Luther King Jr.'s "I Have a Dream," are most appropriately delivered without movement. Do you think Dr. King's speech would have been as powerful if he walked up and down or side to side on the steps of the Lincoln Memorial? Other speeches, like a business presentation in a conference room, call for a small degree of movement. Keynote speeches, especially theatrical Toastmasters contest speeches, require frequent, choreographed movement.

In the World Championship of Public Speaking, competitors make meaningful use of almost every inch of the stage. To make a stage location meaningful, associate it with one or more of the following: a physical location such as a room in a building, a specific character, a point in time, or a key point or concept tied to your message.

Unless you are delivering an elaborately theatrical speech, we recommend having three stage locations. Start and end your speech at the front of center stage—a recommendation we will elaborate upon in the next tip. Then, use *stage right* (the audience's left) and *stage left* (the audience's right) to add meaningful movement. For example, if you tell stories that took place in your childhood, adolescence, and early adulthood, you would introduce your speech from center stage and then literally walk the timeline. For most audiences, time flows from their left to their right, so you would speak about your childhood at stage right, your adolescence at center stage, and your early adulthood at stage left. Finally, you would return to center

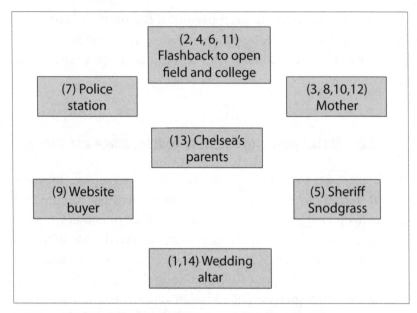

FIGURE 8.1  **Theatrical blocking for Ryan Avery's "Trust Is a Must"**

stage for your conclusion. The same concept holds for geography, where points west are stage right and points east are stage left so that you match the virtual map your listeners draw in their minds.

Ryan set up each character and scene in a fixed location in his elaborately theatrical speech (see Figure 8.1). Actors refer to this technique as "blocking." Each of Ryan's 14 major movements allowed him to relive a part of his story, assume his characters' identities, engage a different part of the audience, and make a significant point.

In Ryan's speech, as follows, we have annotated his significant nonverbal communication. Stage locations matching those indicated in Figure 8.1 appear in parentheses from (1) to (14). Notations in brackets cover movement, hand gestures, facial expressions, and general body language.

# Trust Is a Must (2012)

| Central message(s) | Trust |
|---|---|
| **Duration** | 6.75 minutes |
| Words per minute | 112 |
| **Laughs per minute** | 2.22 |

## (INTRODUCTION)

(#1) [Base arm position; center stage with feet right at front edge] I'm [glances down] at the altar, [wipes brow with left hand, grabs both jacket lapels] sweating in my wool suit. [Gestures with open palm as he looks down and to the right] She is glowing in her white dress. [Base position] Asks me the most important question of my life, [raises left arm, palm up, to waist level] "Ryan, do you promise me?"

## (PART 1)

(#2) [Takes six steps backward while slowly revolving arms] Before I make my commitment, I let my mind rewind like an old-school VHS tape. (#3) [Moves several steps to left and engages new section of the audience] And it takes me back to high school, when I would plead with my mom to let me go to parties. [Bends knees, looks up, and brings hands together as if praying] "Mom, please let me go? [Signals "no" by passing hands over each other with elbows at 90 degrees] There'll be no alcohol, [both hands on heart] I promise."

[Base position] Mom in her nightgown and bunny slippers smiled sweetly. [Right knee bent, left hand on hip] "All right. I trust you." [Gestures to contest chair, takes four steps forward and leans toward audience] Mister Contest Chair, fellow Toastmasters, anybody who has ever lied to Mama before. (#4) [Returns to rear, center stage]

[*Base position*] We're having fun in a field in small-town Texas. [*Reaches with right hand for imaginary beer*] My friend Taylor passes me another beer when [*freezes body and flashes eyes*] bright lights freeze us in place. (#5) [*Moves several steps forward and to the left*] The man behind the lights, [*extends both arms with hands at waist level to simulate a large stomach*] big belly over a belt buckle, [*puffs out lips and points to mouth with right hand)* lip full of dip. [*Looks up, closes eyes, bares teeth, and clenches fists at navel level*] Sheriff Snodgrass! [*Base position, then right hand holding imaginary cup*] Caught us red-handed, [*shakes head and raises left hand holding imaginary cup*] red Solo cups in hand.

[*Both hands on belt and strolls with swagger*] "Boys, it's your lucky night. [*Pushes back jacket with right hand to pull imaginary bag out of pocket; holds bag out in front*] Either fill this bag to the top with cigarette butts, [*spits imaginary tobacco*] or we start calling mamas." (#6) [*Moves swiftly back to rear center stage*] We grabbed that bag, and there we were, three macho teenagers, [*gestures far to right*] Taylor, [*gestures closer to right*] Eric, and, [*points to self*] well . . . [*gestures far to right, then closer to right*] two macho teenagers . . . [*flashes effeminate "jazz hands"*] and me; [*crawling on floor*] crawling in a semi-sober state [*sits erect on knees, holding imaginary cigarette butts between thumb and forefinger of each hand*] collecting soggy cigarette butts all night.

(#7) [*Gets up and moves forward and to the right to engage another part of the audience*] Next morning, we took that bag and we dropped it off at the station. [*Points left to where his mother was in the earlier scene*] There is some angry southern woman yelling in a nightgown [*base position, then turns back to mom and bends knees in embarrassment*] and bunny slippers. (#8) [*Returns to mother's stage location*] Like a human bulldozer, mom plows through the crowd. [*Right knee bent and left hand on hip*] "Son, what's happened?"

[*Looks down, arms close together protecting torso*] "Mom, if you ever worried about me smoking, [*looks up with pursed lips and frown*] don't. [*Raises right hand and spreads five fingers*] The guys and I had to pick up five pounds of cigarette butts."

[*Right knee bent and left hand on hip*] "Why, Ryan?"

[*Looks down, arms close together protecting torso*] "There was alcohol at the party, mom."

[*Right knee bent and left hand on hip*] "Son, I am disappointed. [*Switches to right hand on hip*] Worse, I can't believe you. [*Puts both hands on hips*] Trust is a must. Times have changed. [*Strolls a few short steps to right*] When dad and I were your age, we picked up seven pounds."

### (PART 2)

[*Base position*] It took me a long time to earn mom's trust back, [*gestures to mother's stage location*]; and after a summer of her house arrest, it was my senior year and I became a [*raises eyebrows*] wannabe entrepreneur. [*Reaches down to pick up imaginary buckets with both hands*] This man offered me buckets of money to build him a website. [*Rubs hands together*] New car, here I come.

(#9) [*Moves to far right near front of stage, hunches over and types with both hands*] I spent weeks hunched in a chair, glued to a screen, typing on a Cheetos-stained keyboard. [*Takes a few small steps to left*] I finished, we met, [*hands imaginary object with left hand*] handed over the files. [*Touches coat pockets and back pocket while taking three steps back*] He checked for his checkbook, couldn't find it. [*Base position*] Promised he would send a check over immediately. [*Shrugs innocently and returns to base position*] No problem. [*Extends right hand*] We shook hands; I'll get paid in a couple of days.

[*Base position*] Well, a couple of days passed, and [*raises left hand to chest*] where I'm from, handshakes mean something. [*Holds imaginary phone at ear with left hand*] I called him. [*Face expresses confusion*] His phone is disconnected. [*Moves slightly right and forward to front of stage; extends both hands as if typing*] I googled him. He gave me a fake name. [*Arches back in surprise and *anger*] What? (*#10*) [*Runs back to mother's location just left of center stage*] I complained to Mom, and do you know what she said? [*Right knee bent, left hand on hip*] "Trust is a must, isn't it, son?"

[*Moves forward; base position*] Don't you hate when parents are right? Like one of those annoying hotel alarm clocks, it woke me up. [*Extends right hand to right*] How was I supposed to expect a man to keep a handshake, [*gestures back with left hand*] when I couldn't even keep a promise to Mom? [*Base position*] I learned a promise is only as good as the person who makes it.

### (PART 3)

(*#11*) [*Moves to right*] I was finally able to leave small-town Texas, and I went to college in Colorado, and I met the girl. [*Steps forward and raises right hand to indicate height*] Tall, [*cycling motion with hands at head level*] curly hair, a tattoo or two. [*Shows four fingers with right hand while mouthing the word "four"*]

She is beautiful, and [*points to face with right hand*] I'm just some punk with pimples. After a few hours of laughing, [*gestures with left hand to mother's location on stage*] she is bringing-home-to-mama material. [*Base position*] A couple of dates later, I was upfront. I said, [*looks and gestures to the right*] "Chelsea, I'm not looking for a girlfriend; I'm looking for a wife. I'm leaving the country, won't be back for seven months, and I want kids. [*Opens stance, puffs chest, and puts hands on hips*] Warning though; this, 12 pounds at birth." Sorry, Mom.

[*Waves hands over each other at navel level to indicate "no"*] I have no idea how I convinced that girl to be my girlfriend, but I did. [*Raises hands together at navel level, then expands outward*] We started building our foundation of trust 3,000 miles apart. [*Base position*] I wrote her a handwritten letter every day while I was gone. [*Writes with invisible pen on left palm*] I doodled what our kids would look like. [*Extends left hand*] Dreamed of still holding her hand at 90. (*#12*) [*Moves to mother's position just left of center stage and repeats the "no" gesture*] Decided no bunny slippers.

(*#13*) [*Base position; moves back to center stage*] When I got back home, I met with Chelsea's parents, [*slight fist pump with right hand*] and I got that seal of approval. [*Deep breath and serious face*] I told them, "One day I'll have more business experience. I'll do my best raising a couple of 12-pound babies. [*Points with right hand*] I will love that girl [*cycles hands in front of face*] when her curls turn gray."

### (CONCLUSION)

[*Base position and looks briefly to mother's stage location*] Before the wedding, my mom reminded me that trust is a must if I want this marriage to last.

(*#14*) [*Moves to front, center stage; grabs jacket lapels*] I am at the altar, sweating in my wool suit, and [*gestures and looks right to Chelsea*] Chelsea is glowing in her white dress. "Chelsea, I promise." [*Takes one step back; turns and gestures to contest master; pauses for a moment; then trots right off stage while waving to audience*]

---

## TIP 69: Start and end your speech front and center.

While you can make a rare but intentional exception, it's best to start your speech from the front and center of the stage as Ryan did. There are solid psychological reasons to follow this standard convention. The center of the stage is a natural focal point allowing the overall audience to exert minimum effort to see you. Additionally, by standing near the front of the stage, you minimize the distance between you and your audience. Even in a large auditorium, taking a small number of steps toward the audience fosters a feeling of intimacy. For this reason, Ryan briefly stepped forward during certain scenes to speak directly to his audience, a practice referred to in theater as breaking the fourth wall.

End your speech at the same location where you began. Ryan's speech began and ended at the wedding altar. Returning to your starting point signals to your audience that your speech is about to conclude. For this reason, avoid returning to your starting point in the middle of your speech, since doing so will make your audience feel you are dragging on.

### TIP 70: In stories, give each character a distinct personality.

When you relive a story on stage, give each of the characters a personality, including physical presence and voice, to help your audience visualize them. Consider how Ryan brought each of his characters to life:

- *Mother.* Dressed in a nightgown and bunny slippers, stands with her right knee bent and her left hand on her hip. She speaks with a mild Southern accent softly and confidently.

- *Sheriff Snodgrass.* The small-town Texas sheriff is exactly what you would expect: chest puffed out, heavy Southern drawl, and exaggerated swagger. By conforming to this stereotype, as he does with most of his characters, Ryan was able to devote more words to advancing the plot and less to static description.

- *Chelsea.* Though Ryan did not give dialogue to his wife's character on stage, she always stood just to his right. In addition, Ryan mentioned her curly hair using a supporting hand gesture each time he referred to her.

Finally, note that Ryan acted out each of his characters at that character's particular stage location. For consistency, Ryan also looked and gestured to each character's location when referencing the character during another scene.

### TIP 71:  Gesture naturally.

Just as there is no precise rule of thumb governing the right amount of movement, there is no optimal rule of thumb dictating the type and quantity of gestures. In his highly theatrical speech, Ryan acted out many gestures quite literally, including wiping sweat off his brow, revolving his arms as he let his mind rewind, and writing with an invisible pen on his palm. If such gestures feel natural to you and are appropriate for your message and the venue, go for it. Just do what feels authentic to you and what your audience will connect with.

### TIP 72:  Accept applause with stillness and grace.

In the World Championship of Public Speaking, contestants are permitted to linger for only a second or two before exiting. In other settings, we recommend lingering longer. In business, standing still at the end of a presentation signals confidence in your material and shows you are ready to take questions.

In keynote speeches, standing still when you finish is one of the key ingredients to garnering a standing ovation. As the applause builds, one or two brave souls who loved your speech will muster the courage to stand up, encouraging others to do so as well, since ovations are viral phenomena. While you are waiting, smile and bow humbly but do not move your feet.

### TIP 73:  Maintain poise as you exit the stage.

Maintain an appropriate level of confidence and exit the stage with great poise while keeping an emotional bond with the audience. Even in a contest, your mission has more to do with inspiring your audience than it has to do with winning. That characterization applies to all the prior champions with two notable exceptions. In 1999, Craig Valentine pumped his left fist, and in 2001 Darren

LaCroix did a double fist pump. Both speakers—who graced the stage with two of the strongest speeches ever to be given in the world championship—were lost in their own heads and signaling, "Yeah, I nailed it." However, those fist pumps could very well have turned off the judges and cost the speakers their victories. It is best to save the celebration for private moments after you leave the stage.

## TIP 74:  Dress to relate.

Strive to dress in the same style as your audience or coworkers and one step above them. Most of the people in the audience at the finals of the World Championship of Public Speaking wear business casual attire. Men wear slacks and button-down shirts with a jacket but no tie or a tie but no jacket. Women wear dresses or slacks and blouses. To dress one step better, Ryan wore a two-piece suit *with* a tie.

Audiences disengage from speakers who are overdressed as much as they do from those who are underdressed. The contestant who preceded Ryan was dressed to the nines. He was not just wearing a standard suit, as is the custom for most male competitors; he was wearing a light-gray three-piece herringbone suit. A tasteful fuchsia silk pocket square peeked out from his three-button jacket. Then came the accessories: a fun gray-and-white polka-dot tie, gold cufflinks on his pressed white custom shirt, a lapel pin, a square gold watch, and rings on his left pinky and right index finger. Completing his ensemble were black-and-white wingtip spectator shoes that were all the rage in the 1920s. Though this man was oozing style, his formality and polish created a barrier between him and his contemporary audience. Don't aim to dress to impress. Dress to relate so that your audience connects with you and becomes part of your story.

·    ·    ·    ·    ·

Nonverbal communication is a major factor affecting the ability to share your message. Holding eye contact, moving with purpose, and gesturing naturally all enhance your ability to connect authentically with your audience. Dressing to relate, one step above your audience, expresses respect and conveys the message that you are an expert who values connection.

Having now covered the major aspects of content and delivery, in the next chapter we discuss how to use visual design to make a speech more compelling.

## CHAPTER 9

# Designing Compelling Visual Aids

**TIP 75:** **Sparingly use only relevant props, and hide them when not in use.**

When you read "visual aids," the first picture that probably pops into your mind is slides containing text and images created with presentation software. Creating computer-based visual aids is an important part of the Toastmasters experience, which we will return to shortly. Though not forbidden, competitors in the World Championship of Public Speaking are actively discouraged from using slides and never have. So, we begin this chapter with best practices for using the one old-school visual aid that contestants do sparingly rely on: props.

In most circumstances, we advise speakers to "drop the prop" for two reasons. First, props draw the audience's attention away from you. Second, and more important, props suspend your audience's imagination, the mental faculty you are working so hard to engage in order to connect and convey your message. The rare exceptions to this advice are when the prop triggers intense emotions and when the prop is so unfamiliar that showing it saves a thousand words of description.

Props were a relative rarity in the Toastmasters International Speech Contest until Ed Tate (2000) used a small notepad to simulate a police speeding-ticket book. From that year through 2011, 7 of the 12 winners used a prop.

In Ed's case, he used the prop quite literally. This was also true of David Henderson's (2010) aviator costume, complete with hat, bomber jacket, goggles, and scarf. In both cases, the speakers followed two best practices. First, their prop was directly connected to the emotional impact of their stories. Second, they hid their props when not using them. In David's winning speech, as follows, we have noted how he used his props by setting the references to props in brackets. (Other "stage" descriptions are set in all-capital letters in brackets.)

## The Aviators (2010)

| | |
|---|---|
| **Central message(s)** | Love |
| **Duration** | 7.17 minutes |
| **Words per minute** | 128 |
| **Laughs per minute** | 1.67 |

### (INTRODUCTION)

[*Enters stage wearing costume including aviator hat, goggles, bomber jacket, and scarf*] In 1983, the two best pilots in Texas teamed up to fight the Red Baron. [*Lowers goggles from forehead to eyes*] We called ourselves the Aviators. [*AIRPLANE FLYING NOISE*]

"Snoopy one to Snoopy two, I see him. Break hard right. [*AIRPLANE FLYING NOISE*] Tighten your britches. I'm coming in hot. [*MACHINE GUN NOISE*] Woo-hoo!"

Mr. Contest Chair, fellow Toastmasters, it was official. We flew a bazillion combat missions with zero casualties. We were invincible. [*Raises goggles from eyes to forehead*] So we thought. Truth is we were too young to know that sooner or later, we all fall down. That's the bad news. The good news is no matter how badly you fall, love can lift you back up.

## (PART 1)

I met my first love in kindergarten. Every kid had a job during recess. We were cops and robbers, cowboys and Indians, Barbies and Kens. No two kids had the same job, which was most apparent the one day each year we wore our professional attire to school, Halloween. I had the costume contest in the bag until Jackie Parker walked in, in a Snoopy aviation costume just like mine except she had moves like a runway model. [*Lifts scarf while doing a little dance*] I thought I heard music, but it was just the rhythm of my heart.

I looked at her and my eyes popped out of my head. She looked at me the way my mom looked at my dad after he forgot their anniversary. Fellow Toastmasters, not only was I dressed like Snoopy; I was in the doghouse.

Jackie walked up to me and said, "Oh no, you didn't!"

"Are you mad that we have on the same outfit?"

"No . . . yes . . . maybe."

I learned something that day. Girls don't mind when you show up wearing the same outfit. [*Grabs bomber jacket lapels*] They mind when you show up looking better in the same outfit. You see in addition to my [*touches each item sequentially*] helmet, goggles, and bomber jacket, I had a real silk scarf and Jackie didn't. [*Takes off scarf, extends it outward, then drops it behind him*] For some reason I didn't know then and I don't know now, I gave my scarf to Jackie. She won the contest, but I won her over.

## (PART 2)

[*Lowers goggles from forehead to eyes*] After that we were the Aviators, [*AIRPLANE FLYING NOISE*] and we were invincible.

[*MACHINE GUN NOISE*] But sooner or later, [*raises goggles to fore-head*] we all fall down.

When Jackie fell and hurt her elbow, it seemed like no big deal at first. She took too long getting back up. No big deal. Her arm took too long to heal. No big deal. Until the doctor said she had a bone infection. That was a big deal. The reason why was even bigger. Jackie had sickle-cell anemia, [*takes off hat and goggles and puts them on floor next to scarf behind him*] which meant our flying days were over.

Many of you are wondering the same thing I was. What's sickle cell? It's a genetic blood disorder. People think of it as an African American disease, but it affects people all over the world from the Middle East to Asia to South America.

People with sickle cell have deformed red blood cells which carry oxygen through your blood vessels. Normal cells look like disks and pass freely through your blood vessels. Sickle cells look like sickles. They clump together causing traffic jams which in turn cause episodes. First you're fine, and then you get an infection, and then you're fine, and then you're in pain, and then you're fine, and then you die. There is no known cure.

I'm ashamed to say it now, but when my mom told me that, I questioned what's the point in loving somebody, I mean truly loving somebody, when you know they're going to die?

And fellow Toastmasters, I will never forget my mom putting her hands on my shoulders, looking me in the eyes, and saying, "Baby, losing people is part of loving people. When it happens isn't up to you. All you get to choose is what you do with the time you have. Now that little girl needs you by her side, and hard as it is going to be, you need to be there or you will regret it for the rest of your life; and trust me, regretting is a lot harder than loving. So you be strong and you make me proud."

### (PART 3)

They diagnosed Jackie when she was 7, and she died when she was 14 years old. And through those years I found the strength to follow my mom's advice. Through every episode I stuck by Jackie's side. [*Picks up hat, dusts it off, and puts it on*] And in the end, I decided to say good-bye the same way we said hello. I dusted off my helmet, and I wore it to the hospital. You should have seen the look on Jackie's face when I asked her, "Do you remember how we first met?"

And she said, "No, yes, maybe." And what she did next made me regret ever wondering whether it's worth it loving somebody when you know they're going to die. [*Picks up scarf*] She reached in her nightstand, as she pulled out that scarf.

And I said, "You kept that thing?"

She said, "Not the thing, David, the memory. When my pain got to where I couldn't bear it, I went back to the moment you gave this to me and it got me through. Your love, it got me through. [*Extends scarf out to audience*] I hope giving it back does the same thing for you."

### (CONCLUSION)

[*Takes off hat and holds in left hand with scarf*] Sooner or later, we all fall down. I've fallen down many times since then, but remembering Jackie always lifts me back up. Fellow Toastmasters, losing people is part of loving people, but if you do it right, they'll never leave your side even after they're gone. Mr. Contest Chair. [*Picks up goggles as he exits the stage*]

---

## TIP 76:  Imbue props with multiple meanings.

Past champions have found clever ways to pack props with multiple meanings. Vikas Jhingran (2007) held up an envelope containing a graduate school decision letter and said, "The answer is inside." Of course, this was a metaphor for the idea that the answers to life's great questions are to be found only inside ourselves. Similarly, Lance Miller (2005) used a parking garage ticket that needed to be validated as a reminder that we should actively show our appreciation of others.

Though now completely overdone and downright silly to non-Toastmasters, three world champions used chairs as props, including Jim Key (2003), Randy Harvey (2004), and LaShunda Rundles (2008). Among the three, Randy's was the cleverest by far, since he used a chair to convey multiple meanings. At the beginning of his speech, the chair represented his father's new car—a 1960 Ford Fairlane. Randy, reliving a childhood experience, stood on the chair as a proxy for the roof of the car in order to avoid a pack of hunting dogs that was chasing him.

Later, Randy transformed the car into his new 1963 Volkswagen Beetle, which he crashed through a fence and into a neighbor's fountain. During that same vignette, he changed the chair into a rock near the fountain he sat on as his dad comforted him. The speaker, portraying his father, got on bended knee beside the chair, put his arm on the top, and said: "Shhhhh. We can fix the fence. I'll buy another fountain. We can even replace that old car. Those are just things, but I could never replace you."

Finally, at the end of his speech, Randy turned the chair into his parents' sofa. He caressed the top of the chair when he said, "Their hands always seemed to find each other." Morphing the sofa into his mother, with his arms encircling the chair lovingly, he continued:

> And when Mama was sitting watching TV, Fat Dad would come up behind her, wrap his strong arms around her, rest his chin on her shoulder, and kiss her on the cheek.

Through the course of his speech, Randy transformed the chair into two cars, a rock, the speaker himself, a sofa, and his mother. Randy and his fellow champions have proved that it is reasonably safe to use props in competitive speaking. Just strive to use them creatively and pack them with deeper meaning.

## TIP 77:   Use slides only when they enhance your presentation.

While the only visual aids available during the speech contest are props, the Toastmasters experience teaches members how to build compelling slides using presentation software such as Microsoft PowerPoint, Apple Keynote, Prezi, or any number of other options.

Using slides to deliver presentations has become the norm, but is it always the best approach? As with most such questions, there are two camps, each with a polarized view. Two darlings of the Internet economy, LinkedIn and Amazon, sit in the anti–presentation software camp.

Jeff Weiner, CEO of LinkedIn, stated: "At LinkedIn, we have essentially eliminated the presentation. In lieu of that, we ask that materials that would typically have been presented during a meeting be sent out to participants at least 24 hours in advance so people can familiarize themselves with the content. Bear in mind: Just because the material has been sent doesn't mean it will be read . . . we begin each meeting by providing attendees roughly 5–10 minutes to read through the deck . . . Once folks have completed the reading, it's time to open it up for discussion. There is no presentation."[1]

Amazon CEO Jeff Bezos toes a harder line. If you are called to present to him, you start the meeting with a six-page, printed memo (Bezos is very prescriptive that memos be written with full paragraphs rather than bulleted lists) and then wait up to 30 minutes in silence as meeting participants read, digest, and come up with questions. We imagine the shortest and most successful of these meetings end with a single word uttered: *yes*.[2]

The foundational argument of the anti–presentation software camp is that the effort wasted on design could be directed into enriching ideas. In a May 2012 survey involving 1,014 respondents, researchers Meinald Thielsch and Isabel Perabo proved this when they found that "during the preparation of a typical computer-based presentation, users focused 59% of their time on content, 28% on design, 9% on animation, and 5% on other activities." People in the anti–presentation software camp combine effort exerted on design and animation to conclude that 37 percent of preparation time is unproductive.[3]

The pro–presentation software camp makes a number of equally compelling arguments. The common basis of these arguments is that PowerPoint, or any of its brethren, is really two tools in one. Presentation software can be used as a tool for thinking through what you want to say and as a tool for enhancing what you want to say.

When Jeff Weiner says "materials that would typically have been presented," he leaves the door ajar for using presentation software to serve as a thinking tool. As long as the focus is on ideas worth discussing, we suspect he is open minded about how people choose to synthesize their work. Presentation design genius Nancy Duarte seconded the motion by saying, "One of the best thinking tools around is . . . wait for it . . . PowerPoint. Some of the most brilliant thinking in the world is articulated in PowerPoint. Users can easily associate words with pictures as they build reports, strategies, and execution plans. So don't be afraid to use PowerPoint to create your documents, visual briefs, and other dense content—it's a great tool for all those tasks."[4]

In addition to helping structure your thinking, presentation software is also a tool for enhancing the spoken word. There are a number of sources referencing a supposed study that people retain 10 percent of what they hear, 35 percent of what they see, and 65 percent of what they hear and see.[5] Many of these sources cite those statistics with the phrase, "Studies show that . . ." We get nervous when we hear that language without direct-source attribution. One source cited a citer, a clear danger sign, with "Source: Jerome Bruner, as cited by Paul Martin Lester in *Syntactic Theory of Visual Communication*."[6] The trail gets even murkier if you actually read Paul Martin Lester's article, which says, "Educational psychologist Jerome Bruner of New York University cites studies that show persons only remember 10 percent of what they hear, 30 percent of what they read, but about 80 percent of what they see and do."[7] We tracked down Jerome Bruner, who replied, "I've no idea where that purported quotation comes from." Other sources lead to a mythical study done by the University of Texas. In the end, Charles Fadel of Cisco and Cheryl Lemke of the Meteri Group debunked the whole thing: "Unfortunately, these oft-quoted statistics are unsubstantiated. If most educators stopped to consider the percentages, they would ask serious questions about the citation. They would inquire about the suspicious rounding of the percentages to multiples of ten, and the unlikelihood that learners would remember 90 percent of anything, regardless of the learning approach."[8]

Just how does sharing and then dismantling the most popular urban legend on information retention help the pro–presentation software camp? While the urban legend may be pure mythology, there is support for the commonsense notion that absorbing information through your eyes and your ears should be more useful than through a single sense. In the September 2001 *Journal of Turkish Science Education,* Dr. Naki Erdemir published an article entitled "The Effect of PowerPoint and Traditional Lectures on Students' Achievement in Physics." Dr. Erdemir's study subjected 90 students enrolled in an introductory physics course to a pretest and a more challenging posttest. The students, whose average scores were 61 out of 100 on the pretest, were split into two groups. The control group received normal "chalk-and-talk" lectures. The experimental group received lectures accompanied by PowerPoint. Other than the use of presentation software, everything else was as identical as possible—the same topics were taught by the same teacher on the same days using the same textbook. What happened? Students in the chalk-and-talk control group improved their scores by 6 percent on the posttest. Students in the PowerPoint experimental group improved their scores by 19 percent, more than three times the improvement seen in the control group. While this study is not a perfect test of the verbal-only/visual-only/combined information retention legend, it does make a compelling argument for the pro–presentation software camp.

Some would argue that presentation software is also an aid to helping you remember what you want to say; a more negative way to say this is to call a slide deck a crutch. If remembering your material is simply a matter of reasonable preparation time, then using presentation software as a memory aid is indeed laziness, especially if the slides pose no added benefit for your audience. Though both currently working, the authors of this book are separated by nearly a generation. At 25 years old, Ryan has the ability to retain most information, given a reasonable amount of time to prepare. At 40 years old, Jeremey can't make the same claim; for Jeremey, even with a rigorous technical education or perhaps because of it, that ship has sailed. He can tell stories during a keynote presentation and facilitate discussions without slides; but if called on to present a large amount of sterile information in a corporate boardroom, then slides are his faithful companion. That said, Jeremey owes it to his audience to make his slides valuable. He minimizes the use of text and simply uses each slide as a signpost. Very specifically, he avoids the state-and-elaborate style of presenting where a speaker reads a bullet, elaborates on it, then reads another bullet. That is worse than irritating; it is evil.

In the end, the choice of using the software to present material depends on the audience, the purpose, and the speaker. If you want to inspire, then avoid presentation software. When you have images that document firsthand what you are saying, use real photos instead of stock images or slides filled with bulleted text. If you are trying to inform or persuade, then a slide deck is helpful. It really does take a thousand words to communicate what can be conveyed in one glance at a well-designed chart. Let common sense prevail about whether or not slides enhance your presentation.

## TIP 78:   Storyboard your first draft on paper.

To prevent crimes against efficiency and clarity, we recommend storyboarding your first draft on Post-it notes because their size limits what you can cram in and the adhesive allows you to arrange them on a vertical surface. If you have a decent-size desk, then index cards work just as nicely.

As a rule of thumb, figure you will spend two to three minutes presenting each slide. So build about 12 slides, excluding title and agenda slides, for a typical 30-minute presentation.

You will likely find yourself with too many slips of paper in no apparent order, since your brain is not a linear machine; so think of ordering the slides in the same way you would peel an onion, by starting with the highest (summary) level of information and then uncovering each level of progressively nuanced detail. Preferably, your first slide or two should contain only noncontentious information that your audience is already expected to know. Next, ensure that each slide answers the question raised by its predecessor, typically how, why, or so what, so you naturally build a narrative with a smooth flow.

### TIP 79:  Practice simplicity in design.

When the storyboard is completed, it is time to create digital slides. If you only apply the advice to practice simplicity in design, you will be light-years ahead of almost every other presenter on the planet. To make this process tangible, let's create a slide to accompany the following introduction to a business presentation:

> As you may recall, we introduced Colbertios cereal 18 months ago to appeal to health-conscious parents looking for a whole-oat, corn-free alternative to Cheerios. Fortunately, we have been able to maintain both competitive pricing and high profit margins because oat prices have been stable, while General Mills, maker of Cheerios, has faced higher corn prices due to increasing demand for corn used to make ethanol for gasoline.
>
> After an initial $3 million advertising investment to stimulate demand, we have been investing the company standard of 5 percent of revenue on marketing each month. Our mix has

*also matched the company standard of 50 percent advertising, 10 percent coupons, and 40 percent discounts to grocery stores. Last month, we sold $50 million of Colbertios, commanding a 3 percent share of the breakfast cereal market.*

*Colbertios was enthusiastically embraced by our target customers, given the backlash against the excessive use of corn as a food additive. In each of the first five months after we launched the product, we achieved consistent double-digit revenue growth. However, last month, revenues unexpectedly declined by 5 percent. Why?*

Figure 9.1 shows what this information might look like in the hands of the world's worst slide designer. Imagine further that each of the four graphs appeared with dazzling, animated builds. Let's perform some massive reconstructive surgery to whip this content into shape.

In order to figure out what should actually be on a slide, every slide headline should be a *so-what*, not a *what*. The headline "Colbertios financial performance" is a what that leaves it to the viewer to figure out what matters. As a presentation designer, your job is to do the work for the audience. In the Colbertios story, the most significant problem is the sudden decline in revenue. So-whats take the form of sentences. In this case, a better headline is "Colbertios Revenue Declined 5% Last Month." In business, whether you are delivering good news or bad news, it is best to be direct. When your presentation is well crafted, your audience is able to read only the headlines to understand the whole story. Though we are just working on one slide, the new headline triggers a natural question, why did revenues decline? Your next slide should answer that.

The headline in Figure 9.1 not only has a content problem; it also has a number of design problems. A new and improved version is shown in Figure 9.2. The changes include the following. First, we changed the title font from a serif font to a sans-serif font. Serif fonts like Times New Roman are easy on the eyes and therefore great for large blocks of text. In contrast, sans-serif fonts like

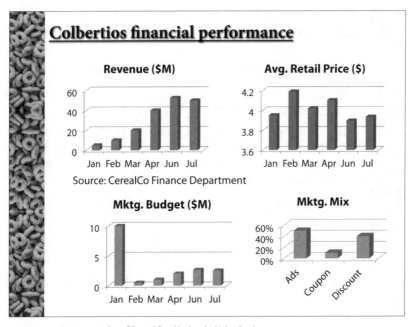

FIGURE 9.1 **An example of horrifically bad slide design**

Helvetica or Arial grab your attention. This is why Helvetica is used on most retail signage and corporate logos. Second, we removed the underline and shadow text effects, leaving only the bold treatment; contrast is much more effective when it is singular. Third, we applied title case to the headline. Title case, or title caps, capitalizes all words except articles (*a, an,* and *the*), short conjunctions (*and, but, for, nor, or, so,* and *yet*), and short prepositions (*at, into, for, with,* etc.). Finally, we added a horizontal line below the headline to distinguish it from the body of the slide.

The slide in Figure 9.2 still has problems. The biggest issue is that much of the information has absolutely nothing to do with supporting the headline and should be moved either to other slides in the body of the presentation or to the appendix. If you do run into a situation where you need to show a lot of data on a single slide, consider the following: While color-coding different types of data is a nice touch, the rainbow effect is distracting. Avoid abbreviations

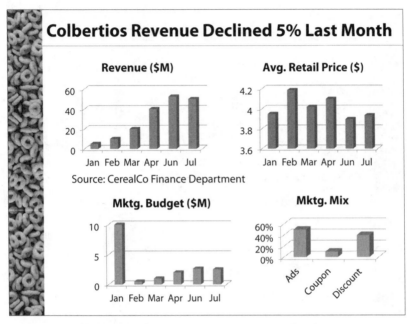

FIGURE 9.2 **A still-horrific slide, albeit with a well-designed and compelling headline**

and acronyms, unless there is no other way to fit the text into the space you have without making it microscopic (under an 18-point font). Marketing guru Guy Kawasaki's highly memorable 10-20-30 rule calls for no more than 10 slides to be delivered in no more than 20 minutes with text no smaller than 30-point font. Our advice is to use fonts that are readable from the back of the room. Finally, make sure to distribute and align all elements to make the slide visually appealing.

Less is more when it comes to designing effective slides, which means we still need to make a few changes to make our slide presentable. The side-panel graphic of Colbertios, however appetizing, must go since it adds no value. Next, the source attribution has been reduced to a microscopic font and moved to the bottom. Footnotes of this type are the exception to the minimum-font-size rule and the rule that slides only contain elements that support the headline.

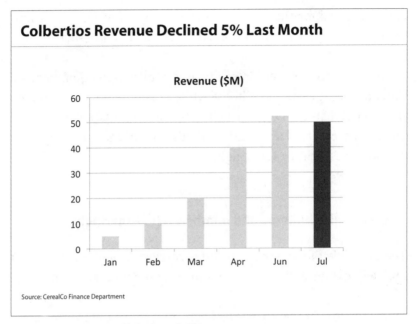

FIGURE 9.3  **A simple, well-designed slide**

Footnotes can provide source attribution, document methodology, reveal granular detail that you suspect someone might ask for, or explain validated but unusual outliers. We also changed the graph to two dimensional; avoid three-dimensional effects unless you are a professional designer with exceptional skill.

As shown in Figure 9.3, our final change applied intentional contrast to the one element in the body of the slide that most supported the headline. Notice that something bad happened to Colbertios's revenue in the most recent month, and so for the column (bar) that represents that month, we used a striking black, whereas all the other columns are the same neutral gray.

Colors on charts have psychological associations. Red is negative, and green is positive. Most shades of blue and gray are neutral. Orange draws attention without implying a value judgment. The end result is a beautifully simple slide that communicates a single so-what with just the right amount of information. It is a simple launching pad for the presenter to review what is happening and to engage the audience in discussion. Best of all, it is a slide anyone can create.

When assembling multiple slides into a full presentation, embrace the minimalist aesthetic. Choose white or solid-color backgrounds that do not distract. Be consistent in the use of fonts, colors, charts, placement, etc. And avoid using builds and animation completely or apply these features sparingly.

## TIP 80:  Use bulleted and numbered text sparingly.

The principle of simplicity on slides carries through to the use of bulleted text on slides. Here are some best practices to follow:

- Adhere to parallel structure, beginning each bullet with an action verb.

- Avoid sub-bullets.

- Include no fewer than three and no more than seven bullets.

- Create bullets that span no more than a single line of text in large font.

- Resist the temptation to spruce up a bulleted-text slide with a purely decorative image.

- Ensure that all bullets reinforce the slide headline.

Just like slides showing charts or images, slides containing bullets should serve as launching pads to present information and facilitate discussion. It is boring and amateurish to state and elaborate by sequentially reading and expanding upon bullets. Allow your audience to read the bullets, and spend your time sharing stories or other essential details.

## TIP 81:  Use column charts for categorical information.

With a profusion of data available in most businesses, odds are that most of your slides will be dominated by charts with only a small amount of supporting text. So let's distill when and how to use the most common types of business-centric charts. If you want to go deeper into this subject, then check out Gene Zelazny's simple *Say It with Charts: The Executive's Guide to Visual Communication* or Edward Tufte's classic *The Visual Display of Quantitative Information.*

Our personal favorite is the column chart in Figure 9.3. Column charts are most often used to display categorical data when you can label each item on one of the axes. Examples of common categories include geographical regions, industries, and time periods. Think carefully about how you order the items in each category. If your items are time periods, then it is obvious that you should order the items with time flowing from left to right. With other types of data, you have a choice. You can order the information either alphabetically or by value. We recommend always ordering from left to right and from the lowest to the highest value—since this is what your listeners will do in their minds if you do not do it for them (see Figure 9.4).

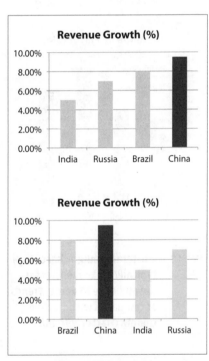

FIGURE 9.4  **Ordering by value on the *y* axis *(top)* is usually better than ordering alphabetically on the *x* axis *(bottom)* and always better than ordering randomly.**

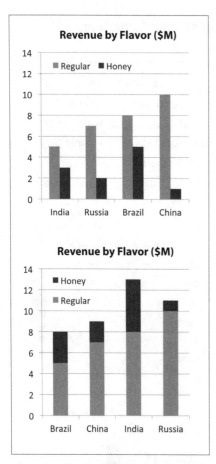

FIGURE 9.5 **Clustered column charts *(top)* typically make it easier for the audience to detect trends as compared with stacked column charts *(bottom)*.**

For this same reason it is generally better to use a clustered column chart rather than a stacked column chart unless the total height of the stack is really what matters (see Figure 9.5). When you present a stacked column chart, make sure the legend items are stacked as well; similarly, make sure the legend items are side by side in a clustered column chart. Figure 9.5 also employs the best practice of having identical *y* axes when side-by-side charts measure the same quantity.

Finally, though charts with vertical columns and labels on the *x* axis are always best for chronological categories, charts with horizontal bars and labels on the *y* axis are more easily read for other types of information. Presentation software makes it easy to change the chart orientation, so experiment to see what is most visually appealing and easiest to read.

## TIP 82:   Use a pie chart to highlight the importance of a single data point relative to the whole.

Pie charts are the second most used type of chart in business presentations. Pie charts are the right choice when the relative importance of the items matters, such as when showing market share. The items in the pie chart must total 100 percent. The main disadvantage of a pie chart is that it only shows a snapshot at a single point in time. Trends are usually more valuable. For instance, knowing you have 8 percent market share may be either a good thing or a bad thing depending on what your market share was last month. Though you can solve this problem by putting two pie charts representing different time periods next to each other on one slide, it forces your audience to expend extra mental energy. You are better off showing the trend in your market share with another type of chart.

A well-designed pie chart follows a number of best practices, as illustrated in the top chart in Figure 9.6. The pie chart at the bottom is the default output of most presentation software; the one shown is from Microsoft PowerPoint. The improved chart limits the number of slices to a maximum of five, including an Others slice supported by a footnote. Next, we ordered the items clockwise by size since this is the natural progression of the viewer's eye. We also integrated the item labels and values into the chart rather than showing a

Note: Others include Competitor A (3%), Competitor C (7%), Competitor D (9%), and Competitor G (6%)

**FIGURE 9.6**  **The pie chart on the top makes it easy for your audience to know what matters.**

legend at the bottom. Finally, we transformed the rainbow of colors that appear in the original pie chart by using different shades of the same neutral color for the less essential information and a strong accent color for the slice we want the audience to focus on. Every one of these changes follows the overarching principle of making a point with minimal mental effort by the audience.

### TIP 83:  Use a scatterplot to visualize patterns or trends in large amounts of data.

If you have too many data points to label individually in either a column or pie chart, use a scatterplot. A common variation of the scatterplot is the time series, where time is on the $x$ axis and a quantity of some kind is on the $y$ axis. Generally, you should connect the dots on such charts. If the data are relatively smooth, a jagged line connecting each point will also work. If the data jump around, fit a trendline.

There are a variety of exotic chart types ranging from mild to extreme that can work to effectively prove the point of any slide to an audience. We suggest you explore the realm of waterfall, area, process, hierarchical, and bubble charts. Regardless of the type of chart you use, take the time to explain every key element in the chart (such as the axes) as well as the big take-away.

For the most part, avoid using tables in electronic presentations, because they make an audience invest more mental energy into interpreting than almost any other type of chart. However, tables are effective and can be utilized for showing qualitative information or displaying small bits of data, such as in a $2 \times 2$ or $3 \times 3$ grid.

### TIP 84:  Jazz up your presentation with images.

Slides consisting solely of vibrant images are now the standard in keynote presentations at conference centers, but such slides are rarely used in business meeting rooms. Your company may not be ready for you to deliver a TED-style talk in the boardroom, but having an image-rich slide or two in a presentation does jazz things up. Just remember, rather than using a bunch of bulleted points summarizing a customer reaction, consider the benefit of showing an actual photo of the person reacting as you share your findings as a brief story.

The more relevant the image, the better it is. It is always best to use your own photos documenting the experience you are discussing. If you must use stock photos, license them from a quality service like iStockPhoto. If you are confronted with choosing between an image copied from the Internet and clip art, choose neither. White space is always a better choice, because the former likely violates a copyright and the latter is amateurish. This is especially critical if your presentation is to customers or other external audiences. When you do use an image, resize it without borders to fill the entire slide.

•  •  •  •  •

Whether you are competing in a speech contest or presenting in a business meeting, props, used sparingly, and slides are effective when they reinforce your message. For all types of visual aids, our best advice is to practice simplicity of design. With slides, ensure that each makes a single point and triggers one that is a question answered by the following slide.

We have now covered the most important content, delivery, and design best practices of the Toastmasters experience, which you can apply to a range of speaking situations. In the next chapter are tips for managing fear so that you can actually stand and deliver the incredible presentation you have crafted.

## CHAPTER 10

# Managing Fear and Anxiety

## TIP 85:  Accept your fear.

The fear of public speaking can never be eliminated. In fact, we contend that the fear of public speaking *should not* be eliminated! Yes, you read right. Anxiety, a natural reaction to stress, causes your body to release adrenaline, which raises your physical and mental performance. So, rather than fearing fear, you should embrace fear as a friend that enables you to speak more effectively.

Speakers often blurt out, "I'm so nervous," at the beginning of an impromptu or a prepared speech at a Toastmaster meeting. Invariably, the constructive feedback they get is, "Well, you actually didn't look nervous. So, next time, don't mention it." These words are not a soothing lie; they are accurate. You never look as nervous as you feel.

Even more important, hints of nervousness make you human in a way that allows you to connect authentically with your audience. One hundred years ago audiences wanted to watch speakers deliver highly practiced and dramatically polished oratorical performances. Today's audiences want you to have a conversation with them that feels personal. Hence, being a little rough around the edges often works to your advantage.

Knowing where your fear is coming from may help you lower your anxiety. At a primal level, standing on stage triggers the same stress response that animals feel when separated from the herd. Even speakers able to rationalize past this can be their own worst enemy. Fear may be rooted in memories of past failures or attachment to expectations of future success resulting from the speech. The cure, of course, is to lower the stakes by being mindfully present; in each moment, define success as sharing your message with your audience, nothing more. It also helps to know that all those staring eyes are rooting for you because your success means that you will have made those people's lives and the lives of the people around them a little bit better.

### TIP 86: Develop confidence in your material through practice in a feedback-rich environment.

Most people first confront their fear of public speaking in their late teens or early twenties, perhaps during a high school or college communications course. Champion LaShunda Rundles (2008) had her trial by fire at a young age, as speaking expert Andrew Dlugen uncovered in an interview: "My mother was a teacher and majored in English. She loved poetry and often used recitation as punishment for us. We would have to memorize pieces and learn to effectively interpret the meaning and deliver it to her satisfaction to get off the hook."[1]

LaShunda had the benefit of practicing in a feedback-rich environment from an early age. Even if you were not lucky enough to have a mother like LaShunda's, you have two major sources of feedback at your disposal. First, you can video yourself and review your performance. Though it is hard to detect issues *while* you are speaking, you can effectively critique your verbal and nonverbal communication by watching yourself on video. When we used this source of feedback, Ryan discovered his filler-word problem, and Jeremey realized that he was not gesturing with his left arm. Second, you can ask for feedback from others. Where possible, we recommend soliciting feedback from individuals with speaking expertise and a style you respect. If you do not have access to expert coaches, you need to learn to separate fact from opinion. When a nonexpert gives you feedback, treat it as an opinion worth considering. If the person's opinion resonates with you as true, then take action. Otherwise, sit on it and act only if you get the same feedback from others. Above all else, the key to getting comfortable with your material is practice, practice, practice.

LaShunda referenced her fear and her "mother's trial by fire" public speaking training process in her winning speech. In the October 2008 issue of *Toastmasters Magazine*, she said after her victory, "People tell me how their lives are better after hearing my speeches. There's nothing more rewarding than that. Most people go after money, but an investment in somebody's soul is priceless." Tragically, LaShunda passed away on August 21, 2012, after a long battle with lupus. Her sister Sonia Rundles generously granted us permission to reprint LaShunda's speech, so that her voice could continue to inspire others.

## Speak (2008)

| Central message(s) | Self-expression |
|---|---|
| Duration | 7.22 minutes |
| Words per minute | 114 |
| Laughs per minute | 2.35 |

### (INTRODUCTION)

I'd generally be off to the side of the stage here with my mom. She'd say, "LaShunda, go ahead. I'll be right here when you get back," and I would take center stage thinking to myself, not if there is a God, but then I would have to sing, "Some glad morning, when this life is over, I'll fly away." I was flapping, but there wasn't any flying. And just as she had promised me, there she was. I had to go with her because I was a bad child and there was no way anyone was leaving that church with me.

Mr. Contest Chair, fellow Toastmasters, and anyone who views logic as important . . . when I finished that song, I'd give my curtsey; I'd run into her arms. She would grab me up as if she had just rescued me, but if someone knows that you cannot swim and they hurl you into the deep end, but then dive in to save you, is that a rescue? Because it felt like an attempted murder to me, but she threw me in that water time and time and time again.

### (PART 1)

One of my most nerve-racking experiences: I had to speak at our high school athletic banquet, and I was eight, and in the tiny little town like mine, that athletic banquet was a big, big deal. As I sat there preparing for that moment, the little voices in my head that speak to me that are usually going at 10,000 miles per hour, they slowed down and all they said was, "You are not ready." I promise you that was the precise moment when my mom's hand was on my shoulder, and she said, "Baby, are you ready?" Then my tongue did something really stupid. I shouted out to my mama and said, "I'm not doing it," and my world stood still and my mama stood up.

I'm five four when I'm really trying, but my mom was five ten, and I promise you, if she raised up to her full angry and elevated height, I thought I was looking at Shaquille O'Neal in a wig. She said, "Baby, you've got two choices. You can get on that stage and say that speech, or you can get out on that stage and look like a fool." You noticed there was a part that wasn't optional, but I learned that day the importance of speaking straight through your fear and right into your purpose.

**(PART 2)**

Over the years, my mom and I landed a whole lot of speech planes. I'd take her directions on whether to go to the front or to the sides, and she'd let me know sometimes when she just couldn't hear me. If I did something great, she gave me a short sweet evaluation. That was good. When I did something poorly, however, I got the full Harry Potter novel version with the witch and the broom included. I asked her one day, "Mom, why is this?" For what seemed like several minutes the only thing that spoke to me were my mother's eyes. She asked me a question: "LaShunda, have I ever told you that you are black?"

"Well, no."

She said, "That is because this world will teach you things that are obvious, but love, love will tell you what matters. That's how I know I have to speak."

**(PART 3)**

Can you imagine the shock on my face when they announced to my family that this rock, this powerhouse, Shaq in a wig, her cancer was beyond treatment. And do you know what she said? Absolutely nothing, and I learned that silence kills. When I speak about lupus, a disease that I have, and it's okay, it's not contagious. I speak in a loud voice because I know that I may not be able to save my own life, but one day I might save someone else's. I believe that we aren't as afraid of dying as we are that no one will remember that we were ever here. I spent four months in the hospital one time, and it hurt me to speak, but I allowed my pen to speak for me. I wrote, one day we will no longer speak. We'll simply sneak to the other side of life's portal, but our words are like seeds that we can sow on this side to make our lives immortal.

**(CONCLUSION)**

Are you speaking and using your voice to sow your seeds of immortality? Are you speaking beyond your fear and dancing right into your purpose? Are you standing there afraid, or will you let the love in your heart tell the world what truly, truly matters? The words that used to scare me so as a child now bring me comfort because I know this much: "Some glad morning when this life is over." My mom can't save me today, but she said she'd be delighted if you would do it for her, Chairman Smith.

---

Developing confidence in your material through practice in a feedback-rich environment will go a long way toward helping you manage your fear of public speaking. The remaining tips in this chapter focus on simple yet effective practices to reduce anxiety that persists even after you have mastered your content and polished your delivery.

## TIP 87:  Eliminate logistical uncertainty in the days and weeks before you speak.

Certain aspects of public speaking, such as how your audience will react, are beyond your control. However, you can eliminate many other sources of uncertainty using the following practices:

- Commute in advance to the location where you will be speaking to familiarize yourself with the route and the duration of the trip.

- Check out the setup of the room where you will be speaking.

- Pretest the technology you will be using and have a backup plan in case the technology fails.

- Discover as much as you can about your audience, including the expected size, demographics, and interests.

Ryan walked the walk when it came to these recommendations. In advance of the quarterfinals, he rented out the room at the contest venue to practice every aspect of his speech right down to figuring out where he would sit and how he would get to the stage and back.

### TIP 88:  Reduce your stress in the hours before your speech.

Even if you manage your anxiety by removing logistical uncertainty in the days and weeks before your performance, your fear will likely begin to spike in the hours before you speak. Consider adopting one or more of the following practices to reduce stress:

- Try to get a good night's sleep the night before by avoiding late snacks or alcohol.

- Drink warm (decaffeinated) liquids and eat lightly.

- Take a walk or engage in moderate exercise.

- Listen to music.

- Relax through breathing exercises, meditation, or yoga.

- Engage in visualization by talking to yourself or to a friend *as if* you had already delivered a successful speech.

- Instruct your family and friends to only contact you in an emergency.

- Set aside two outfits in advance that are clean, comfortable, and appropriate for the venue. Wear one and bring another one along, in case you have a wardrobe mishap.

- Network with your audience (but listen more than speak to preserve your voice).

- Rewire your brain for success by expressing large, dominant body language.

## TIP 89: Slow your rate of speech.

According to the National Center for Voice and Speech, English speakers in the United States average 150 words per minute in normal conversation.[2] During presentations, you need to slow down, and yet nerves tend to accelerate the rate of speech. For reference, world champions delivered their speeches at an average of 125 words per minute. LaShunda Rundles, at 114 words per minute, spoke slightly more slowly.

There are a number of methods to combat the natural tendency to speak too fast under stress. First, take the time to fill your lungs with air every few sentences. This has the added benefit of giving your voice a richer tone. Second, pause for one beat at commas and two beats at periods, which also helps facilitate comprehension. Third, clearly enunciate each word, but make sure to sound natural and not affected.

If you have access to a swimming pool, you can try Ryan's unconventional cure for rapid speaking. While preparing for the world championship, he practiced his speech under water because (a) it is hard to speak with water in your mouth and (b) coming up for air forces you to pause.

• • • • •

We feel that embracing your speaking fear as a performance enhancer is far better than trying to eliminate it. Still, there are many best practices for managing your fear in the months, days, weeks, hours, and minutes before you speak and even during your speech. Knowing the source of your fear is the small first step toward taming it. Control what you can control, and use stress-reducing practices to soothe the anxiety resulting from what you cannot control.

Once you learn to manage your fear, you are ready to enter the championship speaking zone at work and in your personal life, the focus of our next and final chapter.

## CHAPTER 11

# Getting in the Speaking Zone

**TIP 90:** Speaking order matters little; speech quality matters most.

Some speakers get anxious when they take the stage after someone who has delivered an exceptional presentation, thinking, "That's going to be a tough act to follow." Let's look at the World Championship of Public Speaking to see if that fear is warranted.

The conventional wisdom in speech contests is that no matter how effective your speech, you have little or no chance of winning if you are one of the first speakers. Being speaker number one is considered the kiss of death. On one level that makes some sense. After all, the judges have yet to calibrate what great looks like, and the contestants that follow can adjust their delivery just enough to edge out the ones who come before.

Past winners of the Toastmasters World Championship of Public Speaking roll their eyes at us for spending even an ounce of energy on speaking order, but we think it is a curiosity worth examining because of the unnecessary anxiety it causes.

From 1987 to 2012, the average position of the winner was 5.6. With an average of 9.2 finalists per year, one would expect the average position of the winner to be 4.6 if there were no speaking-order bias. The big question is whether 5.6 is significantly different statistically from 4.6, given only 26 years of data. We will save you the pain of dusting off your college statistics textbook and just tell you that a statistician's advice would be for the first speaker not to worry. The average winning position of 5.6 is right on the boundary of unusual but still explicable as ordinary variation.

In 26 years, with no speaking-order bias, the first speaker would have won somewhere between two and three times, and that is exactly what happened—in 1991 with David Ross and in 1992 with Dana LaMon. No contestant who was fourth to speak won in the past 26 years. The fact of the matter is that there is no rigorous statistical proof that speaking order matters at all in the world championship.

Set your mind free. You have no control over speaking order, and it does not matter anyway. The best speech always wins.

In reality, in any competition, you are your own most formidable foe. It does not matter if you are the first, the fourth, or the last speaker. By analogy, view neither your peers as adversaries in your path toward promotion nor your competitors as opponents in winning a new contract. In business presentations, as in speech contests, practice to the point where you are comfortable delivering a message that will engage, persuade, and inspire your audience. When you believe in yourself, you believe in your message and you cannot lose. If you are scheduled to give the final presentation to a prospective client who has already heard 10 others, believe that the sale goes to the one who offers *and* communicates the most value.

## TIP 91:   The rule is there are no rules.

Champion Vikas Jhingran (2007) shared the following when we spoke with him: "People give all kinds of advice like the '10 things you have to do if you want to win the world championship.' I really stay away from that. I think there is nothing that you have to do to win a speech contest. Just be original. Figure out what works for you and then run with that."

His sentiments echo our philosophy—to deliver a championship speech in any situation, there is *nothing* you have to do. The problem for speakers is that it is actually very hard to do nothing. To do nothing, forget yourself and focus on sharing your message with your audience in your authentic, conversational, emotionally resonant voice. When you "do nothing," your verbal communication and nonverbal communication achieve complete harmony.

Craig Valentine (1999) let go of the rules when he delivered his winning speech. At 198 words per minute, he spoke too fast. He referenced a topic, suicide, that is considered too dark to win. He opened his speech with a quote that was a cliché. He ended his speech with a 12-second pause that was too long. Yet, together, it all worked and resulted in one of the most memorable and revered championship speeches.

## The Key to Fulfillment (1999)

© Craig Valentine. Reprinted with permission. All Rights Reserved.
http://www.craigvalentine.com.

| Central message(s) | Mindfulness |
|---|---|
| Duration | 6.48 minutes |
| Words per minute | 198 |
| Laughs per minute | 2.16 |

### (INTRODUCTION)

Madame Contest Master, fellow Toastmasters, welcomed guests and judges. Years ago I had many conversations with myself. Some contemplating my life, but unfortunately many of them were contemplating my death.

You see, as Les Brown said, "I was sick and tired of being sick and tired." I had a dead-end job, a dead-end relationship, and a dead-end life. Ladies and gentlemen, I needed help.

**(PART 1)**

And one day I was in Ventura, California, on the 14th floor of a hotel in what they call the Sunset Room. And I'm watching the sun set over the Pacific Ocean for my very first time as I contemplated my death. And then just as you would take a cookie and dip it into a glass of milk, the sun dipped into the ocean and a few moments later it was gone.

I looked over at the mirror next to me, and it was as if my reflection stepped out of the mirror and walked over to me and looked me in the eye and stared me in the face. I told you I had a lot of conversations with myself. And I looked back at where the sun used to be and I said, "Wow, that was amazing. That sunset was one of the most beautiful things I've ever seen," but I had no idea that the sun goes down so fast.

My reflection looked at me, and he said the three words I never expected to hear. He fixed me in his gaze, and he said, "You're an idiot."

I said, "What?"

He said, "You heard me. You're an idiot."

I said, "Why am I an idiot?"

He said, "Because, Craig, anybody's an idiot who thinks it's the sun that's moving."

"Oh, come on, I know it's not the sun that's moving; I know it's the earth that's moving, but who cares? What difference does it make?"

He said, "It makes a lot of difference."

I said, "Why's it make a difference?"

He said, "Because, Craig, the sun represents your spirit and the earth represents you, and just as the earth rotates and turns its back on the sun and parts of the world become dark, so do you turn your back on your spirit and that's when your world becomes dark; but it's people like you who think that the sun is moving who think that their spirit's moving. You've heard them. They walk around all day, 'Oh, my spirit's low today. My spirit's just down today. I need to go to the store and get some wine and spirits, and the bottom line is their spirit is always high like the sun is shining ready to guide their way. Ready to be their beacon of light, but you've turned your back on it, and you wonder why you have your ups and downs and goods and bads and backs and forths and bottoms and tops and ins and outs; and the bottom line is you've turned your back on your spirit, and that's why you stumble and why you fall."

I looked at my reflection and asked him the same question you're probably asking me right now, "What?"

And he slowed it down for me, and I'd like to do that for you today. He said, "The sun represents your spirit. It's always high, always shining, ready to tell you where you need to go, ready to make you fulfilled. But the earth represents you, and just as the earth turns, parts of the world become dark."

He said, "We do the same thing with our spirit. We don't listen to it, and that's when our world falls apart."

## (PART 2)

I understood this. So I asked him the next obvious question. I looked at him, and I said, "Reflection," because that's what I call him, "how do I stop myself from spinning away from my spirit? How can I always be guided by my spirit?" He didn't answer me. I said, "You were real talkative, Reflection, a couple of seconds ago. Now come on, how do I stop myself from spinning away from my spirit? How can I always be guided by my spirit?" He didn't answer me. Or did he?

I stood and I thought. That's how I think. Silence, that's it. Silence, you're trying to tell me that I never take the time to just be silent and still and listen to my spirit. I'm so busy trying to be all things to all people that I never take the time to be silent. Silence is the key, isn't it?"

He said, "Mm hmm [affirmative]."

I said, "What do I do now?"

He said, "Shut up!"

And I have, ladies and gentlemen; for at least five minutes every day, I'm completely silent and still, and it has changed my life immeasurably. But there's not enough silence in the world, ladies and gentlemen. Think about it. If you're like I used to be, you wake up to an alarm clock buzzing off in your ear, brrrrr. That's your first sign of life. There's no silence there. Then you jump into the shower and the water's running down your back and you're singing a show tune, "I did it my way." I never said you were singing well. Then you get out of the shower, you get into the car, and you turn on the morning talk radio; there's no silence there. Then you get to work; you talk to your employees and the people above you. Then you get off work; you get back in the car; you turn on the radio again. This time you turn to traffic to see what's the best way to get home. You get home; you plop your feet up in front of the television set; you watch *Ally McBeal*, *Felicity*, *Dawson's Creek*, whatever happens to be on that evening; then you get a bite to eat and you go to sleep and start the whole process all over again.

Ladies and gentlemen, like the old lady Clara in the Burger King [sic] commercials used to ask, "Where's the beef?" I ask you, where's the silence? Where's the silence?

### (PART 3)

I saw my friend John just the other day; he was skateboarding. I ran up behind him. I said, "John, you're skating towards a dead end." He just kept going. I said, "John, you're skating towards a dead end." He just kept going. Do de do di do. I said, "John," oh well. John couldn't hear me; he had his headphones on.

But the same way I was trying to get through to John and he wasn't listening was the same way our spirit is trying to get through to us trying to give us everything we want, but we too have tuned into something else.

### (CONCLUSION)

Ladies and gentlemen, what am I saying? I'm saying this. If you take 5 minutes of silence each day, I guarantee you that the other

23 hours and 55 minutes of your day will be filled with a tranquillity, a serenity, a peacefulness you never even knew existed. Five minutes of silence will give you confidence exuding from every pore in your being, and five minutes of silence, ladies and gentlemen, will lead you to feel fulfilled. How do I know? Because I'm still here. No longer do I wake up to my life and fear it. All because I had the courage to listen to my spirit.

Ladies and gentlemen, I want to leave you with one thing today. This one thing is more powerful than anything I could ever say as a speaker. More meaningful than anything I can ever say as a Toastmaster. Ladies and gentlemen, I want to leave you with this [12 seconds of silence]. Madam Contest Master.

---

## TIP 92:   Go speak while working on one skill at a time.

We have saved our best and simplest tip for last. As much as you like to read (and we like to write) about public speaking, you will gain skill and confidence much faster through regular practice in a feedback-rich environment. When you do practice, focus on one skill at a time and run hard at it until you achieve a reasonable degree of proficiency. We use the word *proficiency* rather than *mastery* because it is easy to get lost in the endless pursuit of mastering perfect verbal and nonverbal communication techniques when effectively communicating your message is what matters most.

Even as you improve, rest assured that you will have great presentations *and* not-so-good ones. Do not be surprised if one skill regresses a bit as you work on another. That is normal. When you deliver your speeches, savor what went well, learn from what did not, and, most of all, enjoy the fact that sharing the gift of your ideas and your experiences will make the world a little better for your audience.

* * * * *

Contrary to popular opinion, the greatest compliment a speaker can receive is *not* a standing ovation. The greatest compliment is for a coworker or conference attendee to say, "Hey, I'm really looking forward to your presentation later!" At a time when people have infinite digital distractions at their fingertips, this statement is a sign that you have developed a reputation for authentically and consistently delivering valuable content. When you lean in to your content, delivery, and design, your audience will lean in to listen to you.

# Insights from the World Champions of Public Speaking

Our goal in this book is to deconstruct the speeches of Toastmasters world champions so that you can apply their best practices, gaining a speaking edge at work and in your personal life. We recognize that you may never join Toastmasters. And if you do join Toastmasters, you may never pursue the competitive speaking track. However, if you do compete, we want to arm you with the direct insights of many of the winners.

To that end, we asked a number of past world champions one question, "What are your best pieces of advice on how to win the Toastmasters World Championship of Public Speaking?" You will find a high degree of overlap and consistency in their answers. Here is a summary of their major points across the categories of mindset, content, and delivery:

### Mindset

- Compete for only two reasons. One is to share a message that will make the world a better place. Two is to gain the experience of perfecting a speech through waves of delivery, feedback, and revision. Note that neither of these reasons has anything to do with winning.

- Focus on the audience, not yourself, when you speak.

- Speak conversationally to your audience as equals.

- Work with coaches who have reached the level of the contest that you aspire to.

- Hit the judging criteria quickly and clearly.

## Content

- Start with a topic that deeply moves you.

- Relive, don't retell, one major story and make one major point.

- Ruthlessly remove everything that does not further your message.

- Explicitly state your moral at the end of your speech.

- Build connection by revealing your vulnerabilities.

- Ensure every member of your diverse audience can relate to your topic.

## Delivery

- Progressively amplify your delivery as your audience size grows at each level of the contest.

- Internalize, don't memorize, in order to maintain authenticity and the flow of your emotions.

- Communicate verbally and nonverbally in a manner that is natural and comfortable.

- Stand out by doing one unique thing (but eliminate the risk by practicing it extensively).

# David Brooks (1990)

**INSIGHT 1:  Scale your presentation for the audience and the moment.**

Here in Austin in 1986, I learned from a very talented speaker named David Abel. He visited our club, and at that time I thought, "Wow, is he ever eloquent." He's stunning, and I wanted to be that good. He planted the seed for my growth as a speaker.

Over the course of four or five years, David and I became friends. At one point he said to me, "I have written a speech that can win the International Speech Contest. Now, all I have to do is to find a speech that can get me out of my club."

When you compete at successive levels, you have to grow into each one. In other words you can't take a club speech to the world championship stage. Similarly, you can't take an international final-round speech and win at your club.

Each level has its unique personality and its unique challenges. There are differences in audiences, differences in room setting, and differences in—and this is very important—the maturity and sophistication and experience of the judges. I don't say this to be critical, but it is a fact that there are many great speakers who don't win their club contest simply because the judges weren't experienced enough to fully appreciate what they just heard live. By way of example, Craig Valentine's winning speech in 1999 was brilliant and unusually difficult. He spoke incredibly fast, but then he slowed down to repeat key messages. If he had done it at his club, I wonder if he would have won.

Here is another example. Years ago, I watched a very talented speaker named Michael Holman from another Austin club. I saw him compete because I went to different area contests to scope out the competition before I went to the division contest. His area contest was held in a very small room. I mean, we're talking about 50 feet square packed with 30 people. He gave an incredibly powerful speech. The problem was that he overpowered the room. His delivery was too big for that venue and for that audience. A couple years later, he brought that speech back to a larger room that accommodated 200, and he won. From that I learned the importance of matching your delivery to your venue.

Speakers must adapt to and adjust at each level, factoring in increased audience size, increased room size, increased quality of venue, and, hopefully, increased experience and knowledge of judges. More broadly, you have to scale your presentation for the audience and the moment whether it's in a contest or not.

## INSIGHT 2:    Great speech writing requires ruthless, if not artistic, editing.

Great writing is the combination of word selection and narrative construction. Rick Brunton, for example, delivered in 1998 an absolutely seamless panorama for seven minutes. Each scene evolves into the next, and each has a reason to exist. There's not a word or thought misplaced. His concept was strong. His message was strong. His editing was unusually strong. The problem is, his speech did not win, place, or show. Why? See the comment in Insight 1: "the judges weren't experienced enough to fully appreciate what they just heard live." I contend this was a gem of a speech that was underappreciated by judges who didn't understand just how good it was. Listen to it three or four times, and you'll recognize its artistry.

One of my biggest regrets is that I was not there when Jock Elliott won [in 2011] because Jock and I have been friends since we competed against each other in 1990. He is a superb craftsman with ideas and an artist with words. The great thing about Jock is that he has a deep appreciation for the purity of the message. You don't find any unnecessary movements or motions in his speeches. I was thrilled when he triumphed because it shows—sometimes—wordsmiths win.

**INSIGHT 3:  Compete to gain the experience of perfecting a speech.**

Another observation I should mention has to do with mindset. The absolute worst reason to get into the Toastmasters' contest is to become the world champion. If you are just trying to win something, then go buy a lottery ticket. Your odds are about the same, and it takes a lot less effort.

Instead, your goal should be to use the competition to become a better speaker.

Contests are the quickest route to the greatest improvement because they force you to raise your standards. They force you to play a better game than you can play in your club.

Toastmasters International is smart in terms of having manuals that encourage you to develop specific speaking skills like vocal variety and hand gestures. But the big unmet opportunity in the Toastmasters program is that they should have a manual that requires you to go back and revise a previous speech. And then revise it again, and again, and again. After four or five revisions, you might be onto something. That's THE benefit of the contests: to keep advancing, you have to take one speech, revise it, re-revise it, re-re-revise it until you have something. A good speech rarely happens the first time around.

# Mark Brown (1995)

**INSIGHT 1:  Have a solid message with universal appeal.**

One can be humorous, entertaining, and engaging, but without a message, the audience cannot remember what you said. Your message translates into speech value for the audience first and only then on the judges' ballots.

Contestants often ask me, "What is the perfect topic?" There is no perfect topic. Just speak from the heart. Focus on connecting with the audience, not the judges. Don't impress them; impress upon them the value of what you have to say. Change their lives.

Beyond having a powerful message and beyond being unique in the way you present it, you also have to make sure that your message is one that nearly everyone in the audience can relate to. In the semifinals and finals, the audience is truly international. That means you need to appeal to people with different cultures, different customs, and different perspectives on life.

## INSIGHT 2: Be yourself.

From time to time, I come across people who respect what previous winners have done so much that they lose themselves in the persona of the people they admire. You bring yourself, your experience, your voice, your life, and your message to the forefront. Strive to leave the audience with something of value, and the rest will come.

Some people get the DVD set of past winners and deconstruct every speech. They count how many steps people take before they say a word and what color suit to wear if you are speaker number six versus speaker number three. I did not do any of that. There is a danger in overpolishing your speech. If you go too far, you will lose your sense of frankness and genuineness.

To be successful at the highest levels of the International Speech Contest, you must be unique. What makes you stand out from everybody else? In the case of 2012 winner Ryan Avery, he became characters in his presentation—his mother, a police officer, his drunk buddies. You could actually see Ryan transformed into these characters on the stage. That style has become important in recent years.

Back in 2010, David Henderson decked himself out as a fighter pilot complete with bomber jacket, goggles, and scarf. He reenacted his childhood and brought a very powerful message about love. He stood out with his costume, his presentation style, and had a really, really powerful message.

Over the years, people have integrated different elements into their speeches to be unique. Props were introduced in 1994 when Morgan McArthur used a life-size, collapsible wooden horse. That evolved into creative uses of chairs and ladders. Humor became prominent with 1996 winner David Nottage, followed by 1997 winner Willie Jones.

Most speeches have an introduction, three main parts, and a conclusion. My speech was unique in that I had an introduction, two main parts, and an extended call to action. After introducing the concept of intolerance with the statement that "You never get a second chance to make a first impression," I moved into part one—the fantasy world of *Beauty and the Beast*. In the second part of my speech, I wanted to move the audience from the world of fantasy to the real world. I asked myself, "How can I make intolerance real for the audience?" That was the role television reporter Pat Harper played in my speech." [Pat won an Emmy for reporting on her week spent undercover living as a homeless person on the streets of New York.]

I struggled with finding a third part for a couple of days. You always hear about the "power of threes." In a previous version of the speech, my third example was based upon something that I read in the Bible. Well, not everyone is comfortable with the Bible; we have Muslims, Buddhists, Hindus—every religion and no religion—in the audience at that level. A Biblical reference did not seem to be the best thing for me to do. Then it hit me! Did I really need a third part? That rule is not written in stone. Instead, I choose to involve my audience personally in my call to action. For me, that was more powerful than adding a third story.

I guess that singing a line from a Disney cartoon did not hurt me either in terms of being unique. I still sing that line every day when I speak at middle schools, and the kids have a great time.

## INSIGHT 3:  Use visual language.

Speakers should strive to bring two-dimensional concepts to life in three dimensions. In my speech, I could have talked abstractly about intolerance. Instead, I used the Beast from Disney's *Beauty and the Beast* to personify the concept of intolerance.

When I talked about Pat Harper in my speech, I said: "There she sat, huddled in the doorway, shivering, trying to fend off the bone-chilling wind." I could have said, "She was trying to keep warm," but that would not have given the audience a visual. *Bone-chilling* is a wonderful adjective to describe the depth of the cold. If you watch, you will see that I shivered as I delivered the line. That was all deliberate. It gave the audience both a verbal visual and a physical visual. In the contest, word selection can be critical.

It is wise to have certain language that you are going to use for certain effects. You want to generate an emotion in your audience. You want them to not only hear what you say, but also to feel what you say. Ask yourself, "What is the highest-impact phrase I can use without sounding too pretentious?" Think about that and put that in your speech.

# Craig Valentine (1999)

## INSIGHT 1:  Tell a story and make a point.

In the championship I've seen a lot of speakers trying to make three major points in five to seven minutes, and you just can't do that effectively. What I always tell people who are trying to go for the championship is, "Tell one major story and make one major point." There's an old proverb that says when you squeeze your information in, you squeeze your audience out. If you're trying to get across three major points in five to seven minutes, that's like trying to do a 45-minute keynote speech in seven minutes. It just can't be done, and it shouldn't be done.

If you look at Ed Tate, if you look at Darren LaCroix, if you look at Lance Miller—all of these are basically a story that had one major point. Now Ed had several parts to his story, but it was still basically one major story with one major point.

Most people make the mistake of simply retelling their stories; they do it through a lot of narration. For example, "Well this happened to me, and I'm talking to my son, and my son told me that I didn't do this right . . ." You know, it's all narration. The key to storytelling, and the key to speaking, I believe, is what Lou Heckler said, "Don't retell it; re-live it." I've actually expanded upon that, "Don't retell it; re-live it, and invite your audience into your re-living room." What I mean by that is, you've got to invite them into the scene of your story so they can hear it how you heard it, see it how you saw it, and feel it how you felt it.

Here is another quick example. Did you watch the Olympics at all this past year? Do you know who the oldest person in the Olympics was? It was a 74-year-old equestrian from Japan. A 74-year-old equestrian! My seven-year-old son and I are watching the Olympics on TV, and all they kept saying as commentators was, "He's 74, he's 74. He's a 74-year-old equestrian. He's 74." Finally my seven-year-old son looked up and said, "Well how old is the horse?"

Do you know for a week I couldn't get that thought out of my mind, so I googled it. I found out that the 74-year-old equestrian from Japan was interviewed, and they asked him, "How long will you continue to compete?" His answer was, "I can go on forever, but my horse is 15." I thought—wow, my son's question was much more relevant than I thought.

Let's just take that story. It illustrates a key concept in self-development, which is to never stop asking questions. It is just a quick story about my son and me, but the dialogue helped you feel like you were there. The dialogue is what put you directly in that scene, and you could hear my son say, "Well how old is the horse?" Right?

## INSIGHT 2:    Your foundational phrase determines what stays.

Here's a key to figuring out what you keep in your speech and what you keep out. That's a big part of winning the world championship. The phrase determines what stays.

Your point should be fewer than 10 words so that it becomes repeatable—it becomes memorable. I call it a foundational phrase. The foundational phrase for this story was just four words. It should also be somewhat rhythmic, "Never stop asking questions"—that's easy to say; it rolls off the tongue.

There's a lot more to that story—that equestrian story. My wife was with me; my daughter was with me; my son was with me; we were in Houston; my kids were running in the track national championships—but none of that matters, because none of that really supports my foundational phrase. All the content that supports my foundational phrase I keep in. If it doesn't support my foundational phrase I take it out. All I really needed was my son, the newscast, and what my son said about the horse.

Sometimes you can actually build brands off your foundational phrases. "Your dream is not for sale" is a story that I tell—it's a brand. People repeat it everywhere I go. They contact me and say things like, "Hey, I was going to sell out on my dream, but I remember you said, your dream is not for sale."

## INSIGHT 3:    Tap, tease, and transport.

[As demonstrated in his Olympic equestrian story, Craig begins most of his stories with a question that has an esoteric or counterintuitive answer. I asked him how often he does this and why.]

Almost every time—almost every story. It's what I call, "Tap and transport." In an educational sense it would be called, "Activating prior knowledge."

A lot of speakers start their stories and just expect their audience members to come along. That's a mistake. You've got to tap into your audience's world—or at least into their minds— first, before you transport them into your story. Because then they want to come on the journey with you to find the answer.

I started by asking, "Did you watch the Olympics at all this past year?" I tapped into your world by reminding you of the Olympics and your experience of it. That's important. Then I tapped into your world even more by asking you, "Do you know who the oldest competitor was in the Olympics?"

This gets you involved. You're not sitting back as a passive spectator; you are actually an active participant. People buy into what they help create. So I'm making you part of the process.

Once I tap into your world with that question, I get you thinking about you; I get you thinking about your answer— then, and only then, do I transport you into my story to get the answer. By you not necessarily knowing the answer, it builds tension. I always tell speakers to "Tease them before you tell them." Whatever it is, tease them before you tell them.

For example, in one of my signature stories, I start, "What do you think is the number one thing that stands between most people living their dreams?" People shout out all kinds of different answers. That's my tap. I'm tapping into their world. Who are they thinking about? They're thinking about themselves.

They yell out all the answers: fear, procrastination . . . this and that. Then finally I say, "All your answers are wrong! The number one thing is not what you think." That's not only a tap, but it's what I call, "Tap, tease, and transport." I tap into their world with a question; I tease them to want to know more. Then and only then do I transport them into my story. It is something I do very, very intentionally, and I suggest that speakers do that. Otherwise there's really no reason for us to want to come on that journey with you. Tap, tease, and transport. It's a great way to get into your story.

## INSIGHT 4: Don't just tell your message; sell your message.

People trying to win the world championship have to realize that they are in sales. When I won the world championship, I was a beginner—I was just starting out, and I didn't know that much. But one thing I did very well in my world championship speech is that I sold the message—"If you take this step of having five minutes of silence in your life every day, you're going to find a peacefulness, a tranquillity, a serenity that you never felt before. You're going to finally feel fulfilled." I was selling the heck out of that message.

What does it mean to sell a message? You never want to sell a product; you never want to sell a process; you always want to sell the result.

Here is another example. When I went to buy my first car ever, I went to the dealership, and the salesperson came up to me and said, "Are you looking at that car?" I said, "Yes, sir." He said, "Great, let me tell you about it. This car has this type of brakes, this type of engine, this type of power, this type of window." But my question is, "What is he trying to sell me?" He's actually trying to sell me the car. Now I just said, "Never sell a product; always sell the result." I said, "Thank you, but no thank you. I'm not interested." I didn't even know why I wasn't interested; I just wasn't.

I went to a different dealership on the same day—different salesperson, same car. This guy must have anticipated where I was in my life emotionally at that time—young and single and looking to mingle. [*Laughs*] He walks up to me and says, "Are you looking at that car?" I said, "Yes, sir." He said, "Ooo, you're going to look good in that one. You're going to be flying down the road, the wind's going to be blowing through your hair, and the girls—let me tell you—the girls will be all over you." What do you think I did? I said, "Where do I sign?" [*Laughs*]

He made the sale not because he sold me the car, but because he sold me the result—and he lied! [*Laughs*] I was lonely in that car, I'm telling you. Just me and my payment—that's all that was.

When I was talking about five minutes of silence in my world championship speech, what I was really selling was fulfillment, serenity, tranquility. Figure out what result you're really selling, and drive that home. The title of my speech was "A Key to Fulfillment." The result was built into the title—so was the curiosity.

## INSIGHT 5: Focus on connection, not perfection.

The world championship is not about being perfect. You're going to see several speakers go to the world championship stage and do their speech flawlessly—and connect with no one. Because they're so into what they're going to say, and how they're going to act it out, and doing it flawlessly that they don't even connect with the audience. By the time you get on stage you shouldn't even been thinking about what you're going to say or what you're going to do. The thoughts should all be about your audience.

Right before I take the stage, what I say to myself is, "May I forget myself, remember my speech, and touch my audience"— because it is no longer about me. When you get up on the stage, if you come from that mindset, chances are you're going to connect more deeply than the other contestants.

At that championship level everybody is going to have good content; everybody is going to have good delivery. The difference in who wins and who doesn't is in the connection; and you can feel that in the room. So don't be there for yourself; be there for your audience.

The quickest way to connect with an audience is to share the 4 F's—your failures, flaws, frustrations, and firsts. I almost always open up my speech with a failure story. That way people relate to you. I always tell people, "When you lift yourself up, you let your audience down."

The inner dialogue of the audience members is, "Of course the strategies he's talking about work for him, because he's special. These strategies will never work for me." The key to speaking is to take yourself off any pedestal that they may have put you on, and never come across as special—come across as similar. Put the process—not the person—on a pedestal. Sprinkle failures throughout the speech to make sure that they keep me similar.

For example, if I'm talking about how imagination changed my life, I'm not going to talk about all the wonderful things I've done. I'm going to talk about the wonderful way that imagination has helped me. I'm putting the process, not me as a person, on the pedestal.

Sometimes I'll share my dismal first SAT score with my audience. The reason I do that is because when they hear my SAT score, they say, "Hey, he's not any more book-smart than I am. If he can accomplish this, I know I can do it." And that's exactly what you want your audience to feel.

If you think about my story—I was talking about my son making the comment about the Olympics. I like what Mark Brown says: "Your stories don't have to be sensational; they just have to be sincere." I'm telling a story about my son making a comment about a horse, and people love the story. I don't think your story has to be "climbing Mount Everest." Your story can be about your son and you watching the Olympics—because that's similar, and it's going to connect.

# Ed Tate(2000)

## INSIGHT 1:  Take a risk.

I'm very thankful to have won the world championship; but when I joined Toastmasters 14 years ago, it was never my intention to win. I only joined Toastmasters to get better at my job as a sales executive for a computer company. The founder of our club was a gentleman by the name of Randall Shelton. Very early on, Randall said, "There's this thing that's called the World Championship of Public Speaking, and you need to consider it."

He harassed me for the next 18 months, and it got to the point where I was rather annoyed. I held Randall at bay since my work travel schedule did not permit me to enter the contest. Then I became the training director of the *Denver Rocky Mountain News*. When I told Randall that my new job involved almost no travel, he said, "Great, now you can enter the International Speech Contest." My reaction was, "Great, now I can enter this freaking contest." [*Ed laughs*] Same outcome, different attitude.

I had several purposes for competing. Number one, I wanted to get Randall off my back. Number two, Cherry Creek Toastmasters in Denver, Colorado, has a core group of people who are into giving back to other speakers, and I thought it would be cool if I could be looked upon in that same light.

The year I won, my club contest started out as a tie. We had to have a runoff. As opposed to six rounds of the world championship, I actually had seven. I did something very risky. The speech I tied with was about bullying. For the runoff, I decided I would test out a different speech that my club members said was really good. That was a speech about telling the truth. Taking the risk of changing my speech gave me the element of surprise. The judges were not expecting it, and the fresh humor worked better.

## INSIGHT 2:  Don't talk down to your audience; talk to your audience.

Though I purposefully do not watch other contestants deliver their speeches, I'd heard about a gentleman from India who gave this amazing Horatio Alger story. He literally slept on dirt floors, and now his daughter goes to Harvard. I'm thinking to myself, "Okay, this guy won."

While we were sitting at the table at the start of the awards ceremony, my 10-year-old son turned to me and said, "Dad, I think you won the competition." I said to him, "Son, well you don't know how these things work. You don't know how they'll think, and you especially don't know how Toastmasters think. Let's just wait and see."

They announce the third runner-up. Then, they announce the second runner-up, who turns out to be the guy from India. At that point my son turns to me again and whispers, "Dad, you're going to win this!"

The moment they announced the winner, someone coughed at my table and I did not hear the name. My son said something to me which sounded like, "You lost," and I was trying to explain to him, "Maybe next year." He looked at me and he said, "No, Dad, you won."

When we were on the plane back from Galveston, I looked at my son, and I asked him, "Why were you so certain that I had won?" He replied, "Well, Dad, it was easy. All the other speakers sounded like parents. They were speaking like that guy Tony Robbins." He added, "They were trying to tell you how to live your life, how to do better. You were the only person who just came out and told a story, and it was up to us to decide what we wanted to do with it."

At that moment, I knew I had found my voice. That is my strength—telling stories. If you watch all three of the speeches I delivered on my world championship journey, each is one story from start to finish, and each has a lesson. That's my style. I do not preach. I share life lessons, but I leave the choice of taking those lessons up to each listener.

## INSIGHT 3:  Compete to develop your professional speaking skills.

The odds are so tremendous against winning the world championship—something like 1 in 35,000. However, I'm not saying that people shouldn't compete. Competition makes you a better speaker.

In Toastmasters, speakers deliver one speech and then move on to the next assignment with very little feedback. In competition it's more like professional speaking. You take a story with a lesson, you hone it, and you craft it, over and over to make it better. You get a chance to experience what the art and the creativity of [the professional speaking] business is all about.

Even if you choose not to be a professional speaker, I encourage people to compete so they get a feel for what it's like to hone a story. I literally edited the draft of my winning speech hundreds of times. Testing and rewriting is the only way to craft something that is truly excellent.

I am still an active Toastmaster. I still compete. I always test out new material, new stories, and new techniques in front of my Toastmasters club. I never test out new material in front of a paying audience.

## INSIGHT 4:  Record every speech you deliver.

Now the other thing that our club does is that we record every speech. Video is the best way for you to improve. You can see what works, you can see what doesn't work, and you can see some of your idiosyncrasies. Before the world championship, I went to 22 different clubs and recorded every single one of my speeches so that I could improve by studying the iterations.

Joel Osteen, who is a television minister, does the same thing. I just saw an interview with him, and he said that he has done over 500 sermons in the past 13 years. He said he sits down with his editor, and they go through every single sermon, and they talk about what went well and what they can improve for next time. You should apply that same process of watching your videos and asking yourself what you did well, what you would change if you could. That process makes you better.

## INSIGHT 5:  Be unique.

Before I went to the world championship, I actually watched nine years' previous contests back to back to back to back. The one thing I discovered about the winners is they had something unique that separated them from the pack. It wasn't more of the same.

I can't even tell you the number of contests I've attended and the number of speeches I have watched. I've just stopped counting. The vast majority of speeches I see are more of the same. They're just like what my son observed. Too many sound like parents trying to tell you how to live your life.

The winning speeches have something that stands out. Lance Miller had "Cha-Ching" and David Brooks had "The Silver Bullet." My speech required audience participation where I say "It was just . . ." and the audience finishes with ". . . one of those days." At least 98 percent of well-meaning, well-intentioned Toastmasters were against it. They were saying that the judges weren't going to like it and that I would probably run out of time.

The last part turned out to be [almost] true. The speech was originally 6 minutes and 10 seconds. In front of 2,000 people it turned into 7 minutes and 29 seconds because of the laughter and the audience participation. It was a calculated risk that paid off.

## INSIGHT 6:  Don't speak to be liked; speak to change the world.

For my next piece of advice, I give full credit to Mark Sanborn, who is in the Speaking Hall of Fame and author of the bestselling book *The Fred Factor: How to Turn the Ordinary into the Extraordinary.* He says that our job as speakers is not to be liked. Our job is to make an impact—to try to change the world.

I have a book that someone gave to me several years ago called *The Greatest American Speeches.* In there, you have former President Reagan's "Mr. Gorbachev, Tear Down This Wall," and you've got Martin Luther King's "I Have a Dream," and you have John F. Kennedy's inaugural speech, and you've got Eleanor Roosevelt . . . all the speeches that shaped our country.

The book is several hundred pages long, and there is not one line of humor. Not one sentence of humor. There's a belief that if you want to make an impact, have humor in your speech. There's some truth to that, there's a lot of truth to that, but in many of the greatest speeches of all time, that's not the case.

On the flip side, I saw President Obama's 18-minute speech yesterday at the site of the recent massacre in Connecticut. He was able to make it light at one moment by referencing one of the kids who said to a rescuer, "Hey, it's okay. I know karate." In that very, very serious moment he was able to provide some relief.

I was four years old when Martin Luther King delivered his "I Have a Dream" speech. The only thing I remember about that speech was that the cartoons didn't come on the following Saturday. There were only three channels, and they kept showing this black man who was giving his speech over and over again.

Now, think about the times. Segregation was the law of the land in the South. He declared a new future. It didn't even exist then. It was an idea. He was describing this new future where people were judged on the content of their character rather than on the color of their skin. I submit to you that Barack Obama became President because of that speech. But [Martin Luther King] paid for it with his life.

If you really want to be a great speaker, if you really want to make an impact, take a stand. Yes, at times, you are going to be criticized. But you are going to be criticized no matter what you do. In the words of Seth Godin, you are either remarkable or invisible.

**INSIGHT 7:  Make a deep connection with your audience before you speak.**

I attended a workshop years ago run by Lee Glickstein that exposed me to the idea of transformational speaking. He pointed out that speakers are the most nervous and the audience is the most skeptical at the beginning of a speech. That is a bad combination. Lee said that before you even speak, you've got to make a spiritual connection.

There's a lot of debate about when my championship speech actually started. There were around 2,000 people there. Obviously I couldn't see them, but I tried to connect with each person. I acknowledged them with eye contact during a long silence before I spoke.

The vast majority of speakers start talking a nanosecond after they are introduced. Not me; I want to connect; I want to have that spiritual, emotional connection with the audience first. I know it sounds like woo-woo, but it's psychologically important to me.

# Darren LaCroix (2001)

**INSIGHT 1:  Focus on the process of becoming a great speaker, not the outcome.**

Every time I speak at a conference, somebody asks me: "How can I win the World Championship of Public Speaking?" The first thing I tell them is that simply winning the contest is a bad goal. Your goal should be to become such a great speaker that you can win. If you just create a championship winning speech, what are you going to do with it afterwards? Focus on the process of becoming a better speaker. If I could do anything, it would be to get the lust [for winning the championship for its own sake] out of people's minds.

There are many world champions who have won whose lives have not changed in a meaningful way. And there are plenty of people who have not won and gone on to have amazing careers. So, winning the contest is not the be-all end-all.

In fact, I do not know of too many people who won that actually set out with the goal to win. Consider 2008 world champion LaShunda Rundles—her goal was to get her message out there, and this was just a platform to do it. [LaShunda's message was that our words are the seeds of our immortality. Sadly, Ms. Rundles passed away on August 21, 2012, after a long battle with lupus. You can follow her journey in the documentary *SPEAK*.]

Rather than looking to win, I joined the contest in order to work on the stories that I was already telling in my keynote speech. Those days, I was spending all my time either doing my day job, marketing myself, or speaking. I never had time to work on the craft of speaking. Win, lose, or draw in the contest, I would win by putting those stories back into my keynote. As Craig Valentine says, "If you want a masterpiece, then you have to master the pieces."

## INSIGHT 2:  Build a team, but trust your gut.

Having a coach is important. You don't have a clue if you don't have a coach.

You have to be careful who you listen to. There are two kinds of feedback. The first is "here is what I thought and felt." Everyone is qualified to give you "thought and felt" feedback, though you do need to look for commonalities and not be swayed by a lone opinion. Second, there is "here is what you can do to improve your speech" feedback. Not everyone is qualified to tell you what you can do to make your speech better.

When I fell on my face at the 22 clubs I practiced at, everyone said, "Get up sooner; I was uncomfortable." My coach, Mark Brown, said, "Stay down longer; they are uncomfortable. Darren, our job as speakers is not to make people feel comfortable; it is to incite change." I too was incredibly uncomfortable while I was lying down. If you watch the video of my speech, you will see my foot shake—that was not intentional. I overrode my discomfort by having Mark's voice in my head saying "One-thousand-one, one-thousand-two, one-thousand-three . . . OK Darren, now you can get up."

It is also important to not be coached out of who you are. David McIlhenny was my phenomenal head coach up through the regional contest. There is a joke in my speech about my experience with a restaurant franchise where "I took a $60,000 debt and I doubled that debt. That's right. I turned a Subway sandwich shop into a nonprofit organization." David thought I should take that line out. I said, nope, that stays. That was the one piece of my speech that I had done before; it came from my early days of stand-up but was a perfect fit into the big picture of the speech. I knew in my gut and from experience that it would work, and I knew I had to do it. It is still going to be your speech. Though you may be uncomfortable, you have to stay true to your own ideals. When I won the regional contest, David chose to take a backseat and urged me to take Mark Brown as my new head coach. Mark had been to the big dance, and David was wise enough to recognize that.

## INSIGHT 3: Find a deep message to use as your starting point.

When I got to the finals, I had already used up my two best stories. I thought I had to start from scratch. It was then that my head coach, Mark Brown, said: "Darren, don't write a speech. Instead, pick the most important child in your life. If you were going to die tomorrow, what one lesson would you want to pass on to him?" That stopped me in my tracks. I thought of my nephew. It forced me to dig deeper.

Many people start out trying to write a winning speech. They are not going deeper inside themselves to find what lesson will resonate. I think a lot of people start with the wrong starting point. If you start from the wrong place, you can work really hard, harder than anybody else, and never ever make it.

I can work hard on perfecting a story, but if that story does not reinforce a core message, then who cares. There is a great story, ooooh, it is entertaining, it is memorable, but to what end? You might win your area contest, you might win your division contest, but you are never going to win the whole thing unless you are your message. There is no perfect topic. The only topics that will work are topics that you care about.

It is possible to start with a story. But if you do, then you have to look very carefully at the message. It is better to begin from the other direction—to start with the message.

The gist of the contest is that it is supposed to be motivational or inspirational . . . a life lesson. These are simply universal messages that we need to be reminded of. My message was nothing new. But I put my own twist on it. So, sometimes, we are in the business of being professional reminders. Glenna Salsbury, a past National Speakers Association president, says: "You should be talking about your ah-ha moments. Transfer your ah-ha to the audience's ah-ha." The point is not that you are simply telling a story. The point is that the stories are there to drive home a powerful lesson. Bill Gove, the founder of N.S.A., said that all speaking is: Tell a story, make a point; tell a story, make a point; tell another story, make another point. I do not think there is any number that is the perfect number [of story-point pairs]. I did not have three stories. Ed Tate's whole speech was one story; that's it.

## INSIGHT 4:  Have a no-regrets mindset.

Two quotes resonated in my head throughout the whole process. David Brooks, 1990 world champion, said, "Let no one outprepare you," and Otis Williams Jr., 1993 world champion, said, "Be so good, the only question is who comes in second." I did not want to regret that I did not prepare enough or that I did not follow through with an idea. For example, I had this idea about running. I thought that if I am going to be under the most intense pressure of my life, then I should be in good physical shape. So, I started running four miles a day.

The night before the final contest, I saw a sign for a massage in the hotel. I was barely making a living at that point. My cheap side said, "$70 for a massage, are you kidding?" But my no-regrets voice kicked in and asked, "What would a champion do?" A champion would be under a lot of pressure—so get the flippin' massage. That is an investment in winning. I could not afford to be too cheap to do it. I did not want to have any regrets.

# Lance Miller (2005)

**INSIGHT 1:** **It is not in the winning; it is in the learning.**

I competed and lost for 13 years before winning the world championship. One of the big lessons that changed my life came in 2002 when I realized that it would be hard for me to learn from my mistakes if I was unwilling to admit that I was making any. The audience was telling me that I was not speaking at the level of a world champion. Early on, I wanted the audience to say, "Oh, you are so brilliant." [*Laughs*] That type of thinking was proof that I did not yet have the right mindset.

I learned more from the speech contests that I lost than I ever learned from speech contests that I won. I would never go back and win a contest and lose the lesson. The audience would not allow me to go forward until I corrected specific aspects of my attitude and my speaking.

## INSIGHT 2:  It is not about you; it is about the audience.

I have already had three people in the last month contact me and tell me that they are the 2013 World Champion of Public Speaking. From my experience, if you go into the contest with that attitude, then you are missing the biggest component of the contest. You are missing the fact that the contest is about the audience, not about you. How does your speech improve the way your audience thinks and lives three hours, three days, three weeks, three months, or even three years after your speech?

Humility and sincerity are what make great speakers and great speeches. Your speeches should not be sensational. Humility means you are talking eye to eye with your audience. I see people go into this authoritative posture, talking down to their audience. It comes from watching too many stereotypes of preachers and football coaches. Their style becomes: "I command you to think this way." [*Laughs*] It is better to appreciate that your audience is made up of brilliant people—probably smarter than you are.

I see people time and time again focus on traumatic events. Never mention the word *cancer* in a speech. Playing the "death card" is many times an attempt to try to use sensationalism to make up for other deficiencies in the speaker's skill set. Instead, turn your attention to the audience with a message that you sincerely believe will make a difference. Even if you do not win the contest, you still win because you are actually making a difference in people's lives. The speech that most deeply touches the hearts and changes the mind of the audience is the one that wins.

## INSIGHT 3:  Be yourself.

Just being you is the hardest thing in public speaking. When we stand in front of a group of people, the strangest things start happening to us. You lose your thoughts; your body starts doing stuff all by itself. I want to meet the exact same person on stage that I met offstage, albeit with more energy.

For me, the contest was a journey of self-discovery and self-worth. You need to look at your life and define who you are. We go through life and get defined by our family and friends. We end up trying to be who they want us to be instead of who we want to be. When you can figure out who you are, then you have something of value to give the world through your words.

When I was trying to find messages to use as speech topics, I was so frustrated because nothing really bad had ever happened to me. I came from a good family; I had a good education; I had good jobs. Where is the inspiration in that? This is horrible. [*Laughs*] But I went back and instead asked "What have I learned? What has made a difference in my life that I would want to share with the audience?"

Part of being yourself is talking to the audience instead of acting on stage. Great oratory is not having conversations with characters that are not there, screaming and yelling, or getting overly emotional. It is not about ladders or chairs or orange cones. Just talk to your audience. You should be able to make your point with your speech even if your audience cannot see you. Paint images in people's minds with your words. Share your story with your audience instead of telling them what they should think.

When I bring characters to life in my speeches, I do not dramatize them. I tell the audience what they said and what they did in my own voice.

# Vikas Jhingran (2007)

## INSIGHT 1: Planning trumps execution.

Any time I give out advice on how to win the world championship, one of the first things I say is that in most cases the championship is won long before the actual event. Sometimes it's difficult to understand that.

My background is in engineering and project management, and we do these huge projects in the oil and gas sector. If you ever go to a project management training course, the first thing you will learn is that the best place to influence the outcome of a project is right at the beginning. When you carefully plan your path upfront, the value that you get out at the end is far better than if you rely on brute-force execution.

How that translates to speaking is that you have to spend a lot of time figuring out what you're going to talk about. Once you're in the execution phase, you can only influence the end result so much. In other words, you have to start with something that can win. If you start with something that doesn't have that kind of potential, you might do a fantastic job in delivering that speech, but it's not going to win the competition.

Topic selection is deeply introspective. You really have to sit down and figure out something that moves you . . . that matters to you. It's not, "Hey, this topic will win, so let me speak on it." It's more about where you really come from. What is something that stirs your strongest emotions? Until you are in that place, you cannot connect with your audience. With that level of depth, you can make a lot of mistakes in delivery and still win. If a judge is crying at the end of your speech, then do you really think he's going to mark you down for mispronouncing a word?

Speeches are about the transfer of emotions. If you're not able to manage that, then the audience is not going to have a very good experience. The only time I think you've gone too far is when you are not in control of the emotions that you are feeling.

## INSIGHT 2:  Deliver a moving message to the best of your ability.

I think it is dangerous to go into the contest with the objective of winning, because that is not in your hands. That just creates unnecessary pressure. You don't control that. What you do control is having a message that will move people in a very dramatic way and delivering it to the best of your ability.

I come from a very analytical background. I spent many years trying to figure out how to do well on exams. Though it took a long time, I ultimately figured out that the best approach is to not worry about the grade. You are not there to get the "A." You are there to solve every problem that you can solve. If you prepared to the best of your ability and there are 15 problems out of 50 that you have no clue how to answer, then you should be absolutely fine with that. If you get nervous along the way, then you will do even worse. It is the same with speaking . . . how you manage your mindset is critically important to the overall outcome.

## INSIGHT 3:  Practice idea delivery, not word delivery.

Though I do write my speeches out, I can never recite a speech word for word. I just don't have that kind of memory. I've delivered my world championship speech probably a hundred times now, and I still cannot give it word for word. I just have to be there in the moment and let the emotions roll. The words are close, but they're never exactly the same.

The words really are not that important. The words are a tool to convey emotion. When you start thinking about words, you are hampering the flow of emotions; you are thinking about what comes next. That prevents you from being present in the moment, which is the point of speaking."

## INSIGHT 4:  The rule is there are no rules.

People give all kinds of advice, like the "10 things you have to do if you want to win the world championship." I really stay away from that. I think there is nothing that you have to do to win a speech contest. Just be original. Figure out what works for you and then run with that.

If you are uncomfortable doing something onstage, the audience will know it instantly, and that takes away from the connection you are building.

# David Henderson (2010)

## INSIGHT 1:  Tell a personal story.

When you look at the greatest speakers in history, speakers like Martin Luther King, you will notice that their messages were urgent to the point that listening was not optional. In Toastmasters, we do not have that same luxury; generally, there are no important historical circumstances.

Listeners do not have to listen. Part of what people don't understand about the International Speech Contest is that the audience does not want to hear a "speech"—they want to be entertained by a story rooted in a profound, inspirational message.

We have been conditioned to learn through stories from an early age. Stories help convey information in an interesting package. If you tell a story the right way, you can convert people without their ever realizing that you preached to them in the first place. That is where the power of storytelling comes into play. And yet, when you listen to speeches delivered in Toastmasters meetings on any given night, you hear very few examples of stories told for maximum impact.

The protagonist in the story must be at the opposite place at the end of the speech [compared to where he was at the beginning] to generate emotional momentum. Your story has to go through a limited version of the hero's journey in order to have the real impact.

I went to a Toastmasters meeting in my first year and listened to a wonderful woman deliver a really boring speech about horned toads. When I spoke with her after the meeting, she revealed that she got to dance next to Dick Clark when *American Bandstand* went to her high school. As she spoke, she was beaming and animated. So, I asked, "How could you talk about horned toads when you have a story like that?"

The question I am most frequently asked is, "How can I be funny?" I reply, "Do you have kids? If so, then talk about the most frustrating thing your kids ever did." People will instantly relate to where you are coming from. When you tell a personal story drawn from your experiences, the mechanics such as humor, hand gestures, and vocal variety get automatically corrected."

### INSIGHT 2:  Make sure your speech solves a real problem that everyone can relate to.

One of the authors that I really enjoy is Tim O'Brien, who wrote about his experiences during the Vietnam War in *The Things They Carried*. The reason why I like that book is that he talks a lot about storytelling. He says that great stories universalize your personal experience. You take something that is unique to you and make it something that other people can relate to. If you do it the right way, people forget that you are telling a story about yourself, and they think about things that have happened to them. That is what makes a story powerful.

When people study the International Speech Contest from years past, they come to the conclusion that you are supposed to deliver a light, happy, positive message. In my [winning] speech, people think the biggest risk I took was coming up in a costume; I think the bigger risk was choosing to talk about something I believe is a real problem.

Author Cormac McCarthy wrote that death is the most serious subject we face. He said, if you are not writing about death, then you are not a serious writer. I am not suggesting that everyone who enters the International Speech Contest needs to talk about death, but they do need to talk about a real, universal problem. Losing loved ones in my own life is the most difficult subject I cope with. In the speeches I used in the semifinals and finals, the main person in the speech dies. In my semifinal speech, I shared the story of watching my mother forgive her mother on my grandmother's deathbed for abandoning her as a child. It was about hope, and we called it "The Best Medicine." In my final speech, a little girl gets sickle-cell anemia, and she dies.

When you lose someone, it feels fundamentally unfair. In my speeches, I focused on finding a way for people to move forward from loss in a positive way. Everybody has a story like that. People are not responding to the story; they are responding to the manner in which the story is told. There is nothing even slightly remarkable about my stories.

Often, I hear a speech and am left asking myself, "OK, but what were they driving at?" The message needs to be simple, and it needs to be something that everyone can relate to. In my semifinal speech, the message was "Hope is the best medicine." In my final speech it was "Sooner or later, we all fall down, but a little love can lift you back up."

Now, having a tight message is necessary but not sufficient. The message is the solution. You also need to clearly identify the problem being faced. You often hear speeches with messages like "Dream a bigger dream" or "Live with more enthusiasm," but the speaker never defines why that is critically important in the first place. The illustration of what is at stake is what generates real momentum during the speech.

Last, it is important to illustrate how you get from the problem to the solution. Here is the best analogy I could have come up with on this point. If you take a math exam and simply write down the answer to every question, you are probably going to fail the test even if you got everything correct. Your professor will assume you cheated. But let's say you have some gift—you are a genius or a socialized savant. They still want to see the work that got you to the answer.

When you write a speech, the message of the speech is the answer, but the story is the work. And the story needs to demonstrate the message so clearly that even if the speaker did not say it explicitly, the audience can figure it out on their own.

## INSIGHT 3: Make your audience laugh, cry, and fall in love.

There are very few things I would tell a speaker that you must do to win the International Speech Contest. That said, the one thing you must do is make people laugh. People have accepted it as a universal truth that good speakers are funny. But I think people do not understand the role that laughter plays in winning the speech contest. Laughter is not just about entertaining people; it is about generating an emotional response. And emotional responses should not be limited to laughter.

There was a contest speech I delivered early on in Toastmasters where I started crying. Everybody in Toastmasters is driven to improve their speaking in order to overcome an insecurity. Everybody thinks their insecurity is more significant than everybody else's. I did feel insecure about becoming emotional when I spoke. Funny enough, my original goal in Toastmasters was to never ever cry again.

After the speech, people came up to me and said they loved my speech. I then realized that my real goal should be to come up with a way to make the audience feel the emotions with me.

A little while later, I listened to a man cry during a speech, and I felt awkward. As I thought about it, I realized the difference. The speaker was talking about his experience in the military using a display case of coins and medals he had received. As he came to one section, he just broke down and started crying out of nowhere. If you blindside your audience with emotion, it feels really awkward.

Do you like to cook? Have you ever tempered eggs? The basic idea is that if you throw eggs straight into hot liquid, they will curdle and scramble. You need to slowly bring them up to temperature. That is what you need to do with intense emotion in your speeches—provide a clear indication early in the speech that something bad is going to happen. If I can explain why I feel an emotion through foreshadowing, then the audience will be there with me and won't judge me. That was a major break-through for me.

If you build a speech by studying the last 10 years of the International Speech Contest, you will win the district contest and have a very good chance of getting through the semifinals. In the finals, at best it is going to be a toss-up since most of the other competitors will have done the same thing. There is no way to differentiate between you. If you want to have a chance at a definitive win, you are going to have to be a bit bolder. You are going to have to do more. If you can make people laugh and feel an additional emotion or two, like crying or falling in love, you are going to have a chance at convincing them that you are a more effective speaker.

## INSIGHT 4:  Eliminate risk through practice.

People thought that I took such a huge risk wearing a costume in an International Speech Contest. There are five elimination rounds before the finals [club, area, division, district, and semifi-nal]. Each round is more serious than the round that came before it. By the time I walked onto the finals stage wearing a costume, it had worked five times in a row [David wore a doctor's costume for his first five speeches, then an aviator's costume in the finals]. You don't call something a risk after it has worked five times.

There are a lot of rules that go into using a costume. Most adults do not walk around wearing costumes. By incorporating a child into my speech, it was easier for me to do things on stage that were more of a stretch and still realistic. A child would play doctor and would pull out a stethoscope to take somebody's heartbeat.

Additionally, tangible props also prevent you from having to explain a lot. When I pulled Jackie's [Jackie was David's childhood friend who died of sickle-cell anemia] scarf out at the end of my speech, there is a lot that I did not have to say because the scarf said it for me. Just showing it to the audience brought them emotionally and contextually back to where I needed them to be. They remembered what happened with the scarf earlier in the story which cut out 30 seconds' worth of explanation.

## INSIGHT 5:  Make your attention-grabber realistic, meaningful, and purposeful.

During the finals of the International Speech Contest, everybody in the room is already expecting to listen to nine of the best speeches they have ever heard. So, speaking well is not enough. You have to do something that makes them say WOW! But you have to make them say wow just enough without going too far over the top.

One thing you notice about the speech contest these days is that contestants have this tendency to do things that are over the top. I have a hard time being that far out there for no real reason.

In the middle of my final-round speech, I trip and fall. A lot of people think that I put that there simply to have a big gesture like Darren LaCroix had in his winning speech. But being able to control the time in a speech contest is a major component of being able to win. If you watch that part of the speech, it goes from being very happy to very sad. I did not have enough time to [verbally explain the] transition. The fall made the transition very fast and also foreshadowed that something bad was going to happen. It also illustrated the primary metaphor in the speech that sooner or later, we all fall down.

## INSIGHT 6:  Analyze what works and what does not.

Believe it or not, I was too intimidated to enter the International Speech Contest the first year that I was in Toastmasters. If I had worked hard, I would have had the chance to enter that very first International Speech Contest. I wish I had listened to the two or three people that encouraged me to compete. When I finally entered in my second year of Toastmasters, I made it to second place in the division contest. The next year, I took second at district. In my third year of competition, I managed to go all the way.

Now, I did not have anyone that had won before to explain to me what to do. I did not know there is a culture where past world champions offer help to top competitors. To a degree, I think that was an advantage for me because I was able to break conventions that I did not even know existed. I just went to contests with my girlfriend, Josephine. When I lost, we sat down and thought critically about what went wrong and what went right. We just kept doing that over and over again. We figured the rules out on our own.

Many people think there is familiarity bias during the early rounds. However, when you lose, you have to ask, "How did this person beat me?" More often than not, there is a good reason [having nothing to do with bias] why it worked out that way.

## INSIGHT 7:  Deliver a speech within a speech.

My girlfriend, Josephine, and I go to the movies every single Saturday. Also, we typically watch a show every evening on AMC, HBO, or Showtime. During and after each movie, we pick apart why we like a character or why we do not like a character . . . why a show totally offends us or what it is that hooks us in. Great movies are often built around a great speech delivered by one of the characters. If you understand how screenplay writers construct movie speeches, then you have everything you need for a great Toastmasters speech.

Notice that these speeches occupy only a small percentage of the time of the total movie. For example, think about Jack Nicholson's speech on the witness stand in *A Few Good Men*. The entire movie builds up to that one moment.

If you watch the speech I delivered in the final round, you will notice there is a speech built into the speech. It is the speech my mother gives when I don't want to go see Jackie anymore. Everything else I say is built around that one moment. It gives you my complete message. Everything that comes after simply puts into practice what my mother told me; it reveals how to apply the advice in an emotionally dynamic and entertaining way.

## INSIGHT 8:  Craft stories that appeal to both men and women.

When I competed, I noticed two things. The first is that most of the competitors are men. The second is that most of the organizers and judges, at least at the local level in Texas, are women. Men tend to choose subjects that are not of broad interest to women. Men will talk about getting over their egos, or their frustration with technology, or their relationship with their father. I did give specific thought to writing a speech that appealed more to the women who were listening and were judging. What I did not expect was just how strong of an emotional impact the speeches would have on the men in the audience as well.

I found myself wondering, what is it that everybody can relate to no matter where you are from? One of the first answers that came to mind was that everybody loves their mom. At some level, everybody should be able to relate to that.

# Jock Elliott (2011)

## INSIGHT 1: Push yourself out of your comfort zone.

It is very hard to define what actually wins [the world championship] because I have seen some very peculiar results over the years. I come from a much more restrained culture than in North America. I have always struggled with the difficultly of doing the showmanship that so often seems to work over there. Instead, I have always pursued oratory.

When I speak in the real world as a professional speaker, I cannot do some of the things that seem quite acceptable on the Toastmasters stage. I would just get mocked. However, that is not to say that I don't hold Toastmasters in the highest esteem—I have been a member for 37 years and will continue until I drop. It is a fabulous training ground for learning to be comfortable as a speaker. The problem is that it is easy to become complacent. People can be equally comfortable as a good speaker or as a bad speaker.

It is only when you are forced beyond your comfort zone that you grow as a speaker. Both competitive speaking and professional speaking put you under the gun. Among the two, competitive speaking is the better training ground since you are most directly putting yourself under the gun. The Toastmasters environment has the added advantage that constructive evaluation is the norm.

## INSIGHT 2: Know what you want to say.

The primary thing is to know what you want to say. And so often, people do not. Instead, they fall in love with particular lines; I am as guilty as anybody of that. Often, a particular line or concept is not to the point—it is a diversion. You have to have the luxury of being able to walk away from your preparation and then come back to the speech cold and say: "Yes, lovely as it is, I will keep this idea for the future because it is good, but it does not live in this speech."

Until you can get down to exactly what you want to say, then your speech will lack focus, and you are not going to have a speech of any significance. The old principle of being able to write down what you want to say on the back of a business card holds true. You might not achieve that in the early days of [crafting] the speech. Often, you have to work your way through your theme until it is refined. That can be based as much on your own intuition as on the feedback that you get in rehearsal. Ultimately, until you have that hard, crystal clear message in your own mind, you are never going to get it across to your audience. And of course, then it has got to be a message of value. To me a speech without substance is just froth. You must have something that people can take away.

You have to know your audience well enough to express what matters to you in words that matter to them. The better I know my audience, the closer I am to where they live in their heads and in their hearts, then the quicker I can move them to where I want them to be in terms of accepting the point of my speech, if not necessarily agreeing with it.

In the Toastmasters International Speech Contest, your message should have a universal appeal. Some messages are merely topical; for example, the war in Afghanistan. Current events and many social issues will not endure 5, 10, 15 years down the road. I wrote a speech 30 years ago about a certain type of Australian beach bum. Well, he does not exist anymore. So, that speech only rings a bell to people of my generation who can cast their mind back that far. It does not rob the speech of its value in certain respects, but it no longer has universal appeal.

At the end of the day, only one person takes home the trophy. But if 1 person or 10 or 100 or 1,000 or 10,000 people take home my message, then I have also won. I am not trying to change people's lives. What I am trying to do is give them something to think about; what they do with it is entirely up to them. In fact, in the writing of a speech, sometimes I change the way that I think about life myself and modify my behavior accordingly. That is one of the merits of actually writing speeches. It clarifies your thinking; it discharges emotions; it gets rid of the baggage.

## INSIGHT 3:  Express your true self.

I know a lot of contestants look at the DVDs [of past winning speeches] and say: "Right, that is good [from one], and that is good [from another]. I will put them all together like Marilyn Monroe's smile and Sophia Loren's eyes and all the rest of it and get the perfect face or in this case, speech," but the end result is that it gets very plain looking. Watching the DVDs is fine but only if you focus on trends rather than tactics and personal style.

If someone wins and they have a component in there which is replicable like a song, a dance, or climbing up a step ladder, then you will see a number of copycats in next year's contest. Some do it well, and some do it badly, but they are rather missing the point. Most winning speeches do incorporate a gimmick—verbal or physical—that rings a bell with people. But it needs to be uniquely yours.

I don't do gimmicks, and I don't do props. I work on the principle of being able to operate in total darkness without a sound system. To me, it is the words and the images I create with my words enhanced by body language and vocal variety that should do the job. I draw the line when body language and vocal variety overshadow substance. Because it is the substance which people take home.

In the end, you have to do what works for you. There is no right or wrong.

If you are very tall, you play basketball, and if you are very short, you play billiards. You do the thing that you can do most easily. That goes for your vocal and physical style as well. My "Just So Lucky" [winning] speech was relatively still and quiet, because that is how I usually am. I knew that would either count against me or count for me. I knew there have been rumblings about too much show. I was happy to take the risk because, as always, it's what I wanted to say.

There is one right way of doing brain surgery; but almost every other activity has any number of right ways. It comes down to the person, the event, the audience, even the time of day. So, for example, I can be at a conference, speaking at a rather informal lunch, and there will be a different expectation then, then at the very formal gala dinner later that same night. Not only will my message change, but also my style of dress and use of language. Many changes are automatic. It is just the natural persona we adopt in these circumstances. You talk to your boss in one way, your dog in another, and your mother in another. That is just the "you" that you are showing to each different person.

## INSIGHT 4: Touch your audience intellectually and emotionally.

For many years, I missed the point. I was probably too academic. I was passionate about what I was talking about, but I was obsessed with issues that did not have an emotional resonance. Ultimately, you have to touch your audience both intellectually and emotionally.

I was in Brunei the other week, and a very new Toastmaster said something I thought was so profound. She said: "You are the bridge between your point and your audience." And I think that is very, very significant. I certainly know from years of sales and marketing that if your target customer does not like you, then they will not buy from you. You need to be at least respected as a speaker. Your audience may have no experience of you before. So you have to establish likability and respect and credibility with your audience quite soon. Otherwise, they are saying: "All right, he is just talking at us. He has got this thing that he is saying." If they are thinking that, then you have failed.

I try and put myself in the audience's shoes. I try to get as close to where they live in their heads and in their hearts and start from there. My audience in the United States is middle aged, middle class, middle income, and generally a little bit to the right politically, if you can generalize from an audience of 1,500+. I don't think there is anything you cannot talk about—even sex, politics, and religion—but it entirely comes down to treatment. There is no point in needlessly offending people. I am quite happy to deliberately offend, but I go to a lot of trouble to not accidentally offend. To accidentally offend reflects poor research or carelessness in writing. At the same time, you cannot please everyone. No matter what you do, there will be 3 percent of the audience that hates you. And odds are, they are sitting right in the front row, scowling heavily, with their arms crossed. [*Laughs*]

## INSIGHT 5: Hit the judging criteria quickly, clearly, but subtly.

For many years, whilst I gave very careful consideration of the judging form and addressed all the points, I do not believe I addressed them in the right way. The judges are looking for very particular criteria. You have to give the judges landmarks they are looking for. You've got to address it in a sufficiently clear way for the judges to say, "Right—that bit is done." But you don't want to be too obvious such as saying, "That was my introduction, now into the body of my speech."

As a listener, I am more than happy for a point to emerge a long way into the speech as long it is going somewhere. However, the judges have to hang their judging criteria on a point. They need to see your message fairly early or at least have a useful departure point.

## INSIGHT 6:  Acclimatize to the host country.

Some years ago, I used to come over to the United States a
week in advance and go around to as many as 10 clubs. It is very
expensive and time consuming, but it gets your body clock in
order. Though you are sometimes exposed to foolish evaluation, the feedback is usually very good. Most importantly, it
shows you what is working in terms of timing and language use.
This helps you make sure that your message fits your audience. Generally speaking, it is harder for those outside North
America to compete, simply because we are not immersed in the
images—cultural and visual—that are second nature to most
North Americans.

## INSIGHT 7:  Strive for no audience member to be
left behind.

We have far too many "deaths" in the contest. Some of the
stories are so harrowing and so personal as to destroy the
relationship between the speaker and audience. With "Just So
Lucky," I very deliberately did not have a lot to say in detail about
"me." Instead, I created a series of images which the audience
could put themselves into.

For example, when I talk about friends of our family, I say,
"We had our differences, but we got over those." When I was
practicing, a woman came up to me and said, "You lost me there
because I have family differences and never got over them, so
I could not be with you from then on." What I did was add the
words "But, I'm just so lucky because we got over those." By
saying I was lucky, I acknowledge that not everyone gets over
their family issues. I hope that allowed her or others like her to
move on with me to the next bit. All the way through, my images
and language are crafted for people to say, "Yeah, I am there; he
is talking about me."

# Public Speaking Quick Reference Guide

## Chapter 1: Selecting a Topic

**TIP 1:** Speak to serve.

**TIP 2:** Choose a single core message that serves your audience's needs and interests.

**TIP 3:** Choose a single, inspirational core theme rooted in an eternal truth.

**TIP 4:** Design your speech to have an impact.

**TIP 5:** Talk about subjects you know.

**TIP 6:** Thoroughly research your topic.

**TIP 7:** Respect your audience's knowledge and intellect.

**TIP 8:** Speak with authenticity.

## Chapter 2: Organizing a Speech

**TIP 9:** Use an organizing framework to make it easy for an audience to grasp the message.

**TIP 10:** Use the topical framework for informative speeches.

**TIP 11:** Preview your core message, grab attention, and provide a road map in your introduction.

**TIP 12:** Open with a provocative question, a shocking statement, or a personal story.

**TIP 13:** Use parallel transitional words and phrases to orient your audience.

**TIP 14:** Link the parts of your speech to reinforce points.

**TIP 15:** Prioritize your supporting points.

**TIP 16:** Tie up all loose threads.

**TIP 17:** Call back to your introduction in your conclusion.

**TIP 18:** Summarize your key points and explicitly state your core message in your conclusion.

**TIP 19:** Issue a call to action in your conclusion.

**TIP 20:** Avoid the comparative framework, since it leaves your audience more confused.

**TIP 21:** Use the situation-complication-resolution framework for persuasive speeches.

**TIP 22:** Outline your speech to avoid memorization and reading.

## Chapter 3: Telling Stories

**TIP 23:** Tell stories.

**TIP 24:** Don't retell your story; relive your story.

**TIP 25:** Create a protagonist with strengths, weaknesses, and goals.

**TIP 26:** Challenge your protagonist with a worthy opponent.

**TIP 27:** Introduce a mentor to humanize and arm the protagonist.

**TIP 28:** Craft a high-stakes climax.

**TIP 29:** Tell your audience the moral of the story.

**TIP 30:** Tell stories using a three-act hero's journey structure.

**TIP 31:** Bring your audience into your setting.

**TIP 32:** Build a logical narrative structure by choosing the variety and progression of stories.

**TIP 33:** Adjust the technical depth to your message and your audience.

**TIP 34:** Eliminate jargon.

**TIP 35:** Choose messages with universal audience appeal.

## Chapter 4: Using Humor

**TIP 36:** Get your first laugh fast to release tension, build rapport, and prime your audience to like you and be open to your message.

**TIP 37:** Use humor is in every speech.

**TIP 38:** Crank up the laughs per minute with a sense of superiority, surprise, or release.

**TIP 39:** Remember to riff.

**TIP 40:** Amplify humor with vocal, physical, and facial expressiveness.

**TIP 41:** All humor should further the message.

**TIP 42:** Pause and stay in character while the audience is laughing.

## Chapter 5: Amplifying Emotional Texture

**TIP 43:** Bring your audience through the broadest possible range of emotions.

**TIP 44:** Match your voice, body, and face to the emotional tone in each part of your speech.

**TIP 45:** Express your emotions, but don't lose control.

## Chapter 6: Crafting Engaging Language

**TIP 46:** Use simple words and short sentences to express your message.

**TIP 47:** Intensify your language with vivid images and sensory detail.

**TIP 48:** Encapsulate your core message in a memorable catch-phrase and repeat often.

**TIP 49:** Polish your speech with rhetorical wordplay.

**TIP 50:** Use single items for attention, pairs for contrast, lists of three for harmony, and long lists to build intensity.

**TIP 51:** Avoid quoting famous people.

**TIP 52:** Surprise your audience with misdirection.

**TIP 53:** Ruthlessly remove all language that does not further your message.

**TIP 54:** Build in time for audience reactions.

**TIP 55:** Craft a memorable title that triggers insatiable curiosity.

**TIP 56:** Keep your title as short as possible.

## Chapter 7: Mastering Verbal Delivery

**TIP 57:** Amplify your natural, authentic voice.

**TIP 58:** Add vocal variety by varying your speed and volume.

**TIP 59:** Vary pitch, rhythm, quality, and enunciation to create more subtle effects.

**TIP 60:** Eliminate filler words with practice.

**TIP 61:** Use the silence of a dramatic pause to emphasize a point.

**TIP 62:** Nonnative speakers should embrace their accent and strive for clarity.

## Chapter 8: Managing Nonverbal Delivery

**TIP 63:** Power-pose just before you speak.

**TIP 64:** Enter the stage with confident energy that matches your purpose.

**TIP 65:** Settle yourself and connect with your audience just before you speak.

**TIP 66:** Decide on a base position for your hands when *not* gesturing.

**TIP 67:** Hold eye contact with individual audience members for three to five seconds.

**TIP 68:** Match your movement to your message and venue.

**TIP 69:** Start and end your speech front and center.

**TIP 70:** In stories, give each character a distinct personality.

**TIP 71:** Gesture naturally.

**TIP 72:** Accept applause with stillness and grace.

**TIP 73:** Maintain poise as you exit the stage.

**TIP 74:** Dress to relate.

## Chapter 9: Designing Compelling Visual Aids

**TIP 75:** Sparingly use only relevant props, and hide them when not in use.

**TIP 76:** Imbue props with multiple meanings.

**TIP 77:** Use slides only when they enhance your presentation.

**TIP 78:** Storyboard your first draft on paper.

**TIP 79:** Practice simplicity in design.

**TIP 80:** Use bulleted and numbered text sparingly.

**TIP 81:** Use column charts for categorical information.

**TIP 82:** Use a pie chart to highlight the importance of a single data point relative to the whole.

**TIP 83:** Use a scatterplot to visualize patterns or trends in large amounts of data.

**TIP 84:** Jazz up your presentation with images.

## Chapter 10: Managing Fear and Anxiety

**TIP 85:** Accept your fear.

**TIP 86:** Develop confidence in your material though practice in a feedback-rich environment.

**TIP 87:** Eliminate logistical uncertainty in the days and weeks before you speak.

**TIP 88:** Reduce your stress in the hours before your speech.

**TIP 89:** Slow your rate of speech.

## Chapter 11: Getting in the Speaking Zone

**TIP 90:** Speaking order matters little; speech quality matters most.

**TIP 91:** The rule is there are no rules.

**TIP 92:** Go speak while working on one skill at a time.

# Insights from the World Champions of Public Speaking

### David Brooks (1990)

**INSIGHT 1:** Scale your presentation for the audience and the moment.

**INSIGHT 2:** Great speech writing requires ruthless, if not artistic, editing.

**INSIGHT 3:** Compete to gain the experience of perfecting a speech.

### Mark Brown (1995)

**INSIGHT 1:** Have solid message with universal appeal.

**INSIGHT 2:** Be yourself.

**INSIGHT 3:** Use visual language.

## Craig Valentine (1999)

**INSIGHT 1:** Tell a story and make a point.

**INSIGHT 2:** Your foundational phrase determines what stays.

**INSIGHT 3:** Tap, tease, and transport.

**INSIGHT 4:** Don't just tell your message; sell your message.

**INSIGHT 5:** Focus on connection, not perfection.

## Ed Tate (2000)

**INSIGHT 1:** Take a risk.

**INSIGHT 2:** Don't talk down to your audience; talk to your audience.

**INSIGHT 3:** Compete to develop your professional speaking skills.

**INSIGHT 4:** Record every speech you deliver.

**INSIGHT 5:** Be unique.

**INSIGHT 6:** Don't speak to be liked; speak to change the world.

**INSIGHT 7:** Make a deep connection with your audience before you speak.

## Darren LaCroix (2001)

**INSIGHT 1:** Focus on the process of becoming a great speaker, not the outcome.

**INSIGHT 2:** Build a team, but trust your gut.

**INSIGHT 3:** Find a deep message to use as your starting point.

**INSIGHT 4:** Have a no-regrets mindset.

### Lance Miller (2005)

**INSIGHT 1:** It is not in the winning; it is in the learning.

**INSIGHT 2:** It is not about you; it is about the audience.

**INSIGHT 3:** Be yourself.

### Vikas Jhingran (2007)

**INSIGHT 1:** Planning trumps execution.

**INSIGHT 2:** Deliver a moving message to the best of your ability.

**INSIGHT 3:** Practice idea delivery, not word delivery.

**INSIGHT 4:** The rule is there are no rules.

### David Henderson (2010)

**INSIGHT 1:** Tell a personal story.

**INSIGHT 2:** Make sure your speech solves a real problem that everyone can relate to.

**INSIGHT 3:** Make your audience laugh, cry, and fall in love.

**INSIGHT 4:** Eliminate risk through practice.

**INSIGHT 5:** Make your attention-grabber realistic, meaningful, and purposeful.

**INSIGHT 6:** Analyze what works and what does not.

**INSIGHT 7:** Deliver a speech within a speech.

**INSIGHT 8:** Craft stories that appeal to both men and women.

## Jock Elliott (2011)

**INSIGHT 1:** Push yourself out of your comfort zone.

**INSIGHT 2:** Know what you want to say.

**INSIGHT 3:** Express your true self.

**INSIGHT 4:** Touch your audience intellectually and emotionally.

**INSIGHT 5:** Hit the judging criteria quickly, clearly, but subtly.

**INSIGHT 6:** Acclimatize to the host country.

**INSIGHT 7:** Strive for no audience member to be left behind.

# NOTES

## Introduction

1. http://www.toastmasters.org/toastmastersmagazine/toastmasterarchive/2007/november/the3rs.aspx.

## Chapter 1

1. http://www.guardian.co.uk/world/2007/apr/23/nelsonmandela1.

## Chapter 3

1. Nicole Speer, Jeremy R. Reynolds, Khena M. Swallow, and Jeffrey Zachs. "Reading Stories Activates Neural Representations of Visual and Motor Experiences." *Psychological Science*, August 2009, vol. 20, no.8, pp. 989–999.
2. Goran Stojkovic, Francois Soumis, Jacques Desrosiers, and Marius M. Solomon. "An Optimization Model for a Real-Time Flight Scheduling Problem." *Transportation Research Part A*, 2002, vol. 36, pp. 779–788.
3. http://www.cdc.gov/ncbddd/sicklecell/data.html.

## Chapter 4

1. Toastmasters familiar with the contest will wonder why Darren was not disqualified for going over the 7-minute, 30-second time limit. According to Darren, there was a timing light malfunction, granting him an extra 30 seconds per the contest rules.

## Chapter 6

1. Sir Arthur Quiller-Couch. "On Style." *On the Art of Writing,* 1916, Section XII.
2. http://blog.hubspot.com/blog/tabid/6307/bid/33982/HubSpot-s-10-Hottest-Marketing-Blog-Posts-of-2012.aspx.

## Chapter 8

1. Italics added. Dana R. Carney, Amy J. C. Cuddy, and Andy J. Yap. "Power Posing: Brief Nonverbal Displays Affect Neuroendocrine Levels and Risk Tolerance." *Psychological Science*, 2010, vol. 21, no. 10, pp. 1363–1368, http://faculty.haas.berkeley.edu/dana_carney/power.poses.PS.2010.pdf.

## Chapter 9

1. http://www.linkedin.com/today/post/article/20130701022638-22330283-a-simple-rule-to-eliminate-useless-meetings?trk=tod-posts-art-.
2. http://management.fortune.cnn.com/2012/11/16/jeff-bezos-amazon.
3. http://techcomm.stc.org/wp-content/uploads/2012/06/2Perabo_TecComm_May_2ndQRT_2012.pdf.
4. http://www.linkedin.com/today/post/article/20130729191149-172811-present-slides-distribute-documents.
5. https://www.osha.gov/doc/outreachtraining/htmlfiles/traintec.html.
6. http://www.hp.com/large/ipg/assets/bus-solutions/power-of-visual-communication.pdf.
7. http://commfaculty.fullerton.edu/lester/writings/viscomtheory.html.
8. http://www.cisco.com/web/strategy/docs/education/Multimodal-Learning-Through-Media.pdf.

## Chapter 10

1. http://sixminutes.dlugan.com/lashunda-rundles-2008-world-champion-public-speaking.
2. http://www.ncvs.org/ncvs/tutorials/voiceprod/tutorial/quality.html.

# INDEX

Note: page numbers in **bold** indicate speeches by Toastmaster Champions; years in parentheses indicate the year the Championship was won.

Jeremey Donovan is group vice president of marketing at Gartner, Inc., the world's leading information technology research and advisory company with $1.6 billion in annual revenue. During his career, Jeremey has led successful teams focused on market research, new product development, marketing, acquisitions, and product management. He is a Distinguished Toastmaster, a three-time TEDx organizer, a TEDx speaker, and a public speaking coach. He is the bestselling author of *How to Deliver a TED Talk* and *What Great Looks Like*. Please visit http://www.speakingsherpa.com for more information.

Ryan Avery is the 2012 World Champion of Public Speaking, and at 25, the youngest in history. An Emmy Award–winning journalist, he delivers keynotes and workshops designed to help aspiring speakers craft and deliver their message. Please visit http://www .howtobeaspeaker.com and http://www.averytoday.com for more information.

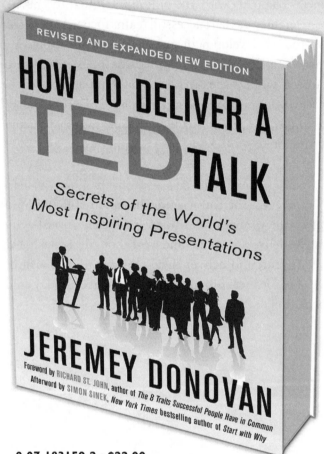